Lowestoft Fishing Vessels Rememb[ered]
Wrecked, Sunk and Missing Vessels of the Lowestoft Fleet 1939-91

by
Malcolm R. White

Lowestoft Fishing Vessels Remembered

GENERAL INFORMATION

BOOK DETAILS

Published by Malcolm R. White
Coastal Publications
71 Beeching Drive
Lowestoft
NR32 4TB
First Published December 2013
Copyright © Malcolm R. White 2013

Printed by Micropress Printers Ltd.
Fountain Way
Reydon Business Park
Reydon
IP18 6DH
ISBN 978-0-9575672-0-7
All rights reserved

THIS PUBLICATION

Every effort has been made to ensure that information contained in this publication is accurate and for this reason many sources have been consulted. These include official documentation, local diaries, media and enthusiasts resources and numerous accredited research works. However, when considering such a complex subject with some details gathered from records that were provided by other parties, 100% accuracy is difficult to guarantee. Books in this series are part of the National Published Archive and as such are included in the library collections of the British Library, the National Library of Scotland, the National Library of Wales, the Universities of Oxford and Cambridge, Trinity College, Dublin and, when appropriate, The National Museum of Science & Industry. This series is published on a non profit basis and not, as in the great majority of similar works, for financial gain of the author(s) and a commercial publisher. Any profit that does arise from the sale of books in this series is donated discreetly to charity and good causes.

PHOTOGRAPHIC OWNERSHIP AND COPYRIGHT

No part of this publication may be reproduced, stored in a retrieval system, or transmitted in any form or by any means electronic, mechanical, photocopying, recording or otherwise, without the express permission of the Publisher and the Copyright holder in writing.

ACKNOWLEDGEMENTS

The following past and present organisations have assisted either directly or indirectly in this publication by providing research and photographic material : - Banffshire Maritime and Heritage Association, Lowestoft Record Office, Lowestoft & East Suffolk Maritime Society, Port of Lowestoft Research Society, Colne Shipping Co. Ltd. [circa 1999], Cromer RNLI [circa 2000], Richards Shipbuilders Ltd. [circa1992] and Small & Co. (Lowestoft) Ltd. [circa 2001]. Several maritime and heritage enthusiasts have assisted with this project in many ways and these include :- Mr. Ivan Bunn, Mr. Peter Calvert, the late Mr. Tom Drew, Mr. Stanley Earl, Pamela Graystone, Mr. Peter Hansford, the late Mr. Ernest Harvey, the late Mr. Ken Kent, Mr. James A. Pottinger Mr. Parry Watson, Mr. John Wells and Mrs. Cathryn White.

Numerous reference sources have been consulted during the preparation of this book including the Lloyds Register of Ships, various Olsen's Nautical Almanacks, the Lowestoft Fishing Vessel Database, various war memorials, the European Commission Fleet Register of Fishing Vessels, various newspaper and other media reports, Hansard, on line sources covering the history of the Royal Navy in World War II, and the minutes of various courts of inquiry into ship losses.

I am most grateful for the considerable assistance provided by Mr. Peter Killby in supplying photographs, information and much historical data regarding the life and times of many of the vessels featured in this work.

Successful completion of *Lowestoft Fishing Vessels Remembered* would not have been possible without the valuable help provided by Mr. Stuart Jones BA. Stuart has provided important editorial support for the previous twenty titles in this series and has done so again with this latest addition.

CAPTIONS

Front Cover Top Left - TH35 *Pescado* leaves on a fishing trip. *[Copyright Stanley Earl]*
Bottom Left - LT526 *Devon County* approaches the Lowestoft pier heads from sea. *[Malcolm White Collection]*
Bottom Right - LO488 *Susan M.* approaches the Lowestoft pier heads from sea. *[Courtesy Small & Co. (Lowestoft) Ltd.]*
Title Page LT432 *Boston Pionair* approaches the Lowestoft pier heads from sea. *[Richards Shipbuilders - Cyril Richards Archive]*
Page Three R116 *Nikki* leaves on a fishing trip *[Courtesy Ken Kent (circa 1997)]*

Lowestoft Fishing Vessels Remembered

CONTENTS

		PAGE
Introduction		4
Section One 1939 - 1945	Summary of Lowestoft Requisitioned and Fishing Vessel Casualties	5
	Photographic Selection	8
Section Two 1946 - 1991	Details of Lowestoft Fishing and former Fishing Vessel Casualties	11
	The Admiralty "standard" drifter and MFVs	12
	Details of Individual Vessels with Photographs	13
Section Three	A selection of other Lowestoft Fishing Vessel Casualties with Photographs	114

Introduction

Following the decline and eventual cessation of fishing by trawlers and drifters of the Lowestoft fleet towards the end of the 20th century, the fishing industry no longer enjoys the high profile it once had in the economic fortunes of the town. Today (2013) a number of small fishing vessels operate from the port where a much reduced fish market is still very active. The remaining fishing industry has a much lower profile following the disappearance of large trawlers from the harbour and consequently, 21st century visitors and many of the townsfolk may not appreciate the enormous sacrifice made by our fishing vessel crews. Over many years fishing vessels, large and small, have been lost in peacetime and in war with the loss of part or all of the crew.

A neglected and important aspect of the life of the town has been the work of the Lowestoft fishing fleet during wartime. A large number of Lowestoft vessels were requisitioned by the naval authorities during the Second World War for a wide variety of duties including minesweeping. Several vessels were destroyed or severely damaged by enemy action including mines, gunfire or being bombed, with the result that many crew members lost their lives or were injured; other vessels on naval service were lost due to collisions or sustained damaged whilst at work in British waters again with casualties amongst the crews. Several Lowestoft vessels that were not requisitioned carried on with their normal fishing work mainly off the west coast. However, they were often attacked there by gunfire or bombs from enemy aircraft.

In peacetime, the most memorable and drastic losses have been when a Lowestoft vessel fails to return to the safety of the port after being subjected to extreme sea conditions or has been destroyed by a wartime mine or similar explosive device, many years after the end of hostilities. Whatever the cause of the loss, many fishermen have lost their lives.

No book or research work has collectively featured the vessels from the port of Lowestoft that have been deleted from the town's once great fishing fleet due to being wrecked, sinking, explosions, fire damage, or in World War II by enemy action. The purpose of this book is to remember those Lowestoft fishing vessels that have been lost since 1939, and where applicable, remember any crew member lost since 1946 as a consequence of their drifter or trawler coming to an unexpected end.

Neglected for so long, hopefully this book will start to rectify an important shortcoming in the many already published works relating to bygone Lowestoft.

Malcolm White
Lowestoft
November 2013

Lowestoft Fishing Vessel Casualties 1939 - 1945.

A selection of Lowestoft owned or registered vessels lost or badly damaged whilst undertaking naval duties or commercial fishing activities between 1939 and 1945.

Information

The vessels listed in this section were either undertaking normal commercial fishing activities or naval duties after being requisitioned, leased or purchased by the Admiralty. In a very few cases some of those listed may have been salvaged for breaking up or repair. The list includes drifters, trawlers, drifter/trawlers and motorised sailing smacks.

It is possible that not all vessels lost between 1939 and 1945 which had associations with the port of Lowestoft are included. However, following intensive research it is hoped that very few casualties have gone unnoticed. In many of the incidents listed, crew members lost their lives and in some cases, the entire crew were lost. An example of this was the destruction of the Lowestoft trawler *Hopton* by a mine off Iceland when Skipper W. Bensley and ten crew members lost their lives.

The vessels are shown with their peacetime fishing registration and name. Those under Admiralty control were given naval identities and in most cases this did include the peacetime name. The photographs included in this section are a representation of the types of vessels known to have been lost.

The Lowestoft trawler *Aberdeen* was attacked by enemy aircraft on Tuesday March 11th 1941 with bombs and gunfire whilst fishing in Cardigan Bay. As result of this action, Third Hand Arthur Butler, Chief Engineer Frederick E. Catchpole, Third Engineer Leslie Harrison, Stoker William T. Mills, Second Engineer James A. Murphy and Cook Henry G. Page all lost their lives.
[Photograph from the Malcolm White Collection]

Lowestoft Fishing Vessel Casualties 1939 - 1945

Date		Vessel	Cause of loss
1939	December 10th	LT230 *Ray of Hope*	Mined and sank in the Thames Estuary.
1940	January 6th	LT57 *Eta*	Mined and sank in the vicinity of the Outer Gabbard Light Vessel.
	January 15th	LT134 *Newhaven*	Mined and sank off Suffolk coast.
	March 11th	LT144 *Halifax*	Mined and sank off Suffolk coast.
	March 16th	LT138 *Xania*	Sank following a collision with LT123 *Aberdeen* off the Welsh coast.
	March 30th	LT279 *Walsingham*	Sank following a collision approximately 25 miles SE of Harwich, whilst on passage from Grimsby to Milford Haven. Actual sinking recorded as "on or about the 30th - 31st March".
	May 28th	LT1167 *Boy Roy*	Bombed and beached at Dunkirk.
	May 28th	LT1114 *Paxton*	Damaged by aircraft, and beached at Dunkirk.
	May 29th	LT52 *Girl Pamela*	Sank following a collision off Dunkirk.
	June 1st	YH65 *Fairbreeze*	Lost at Dunkirk after striking a submerged wreck. (Lowestoft owned vessel)
	June 2nd	LT680 *Lord Cavan*	Sunk by gunfire off Dunkirk, date of sinking recorded as "on or about 2nd June".
	August 10th	LT1175 *Young Sid*	Sank following a collision in the Moray Firth, Scotland.
	August 18th	LT156 *Valeria*	Bombed by aircraft and sank off St. David's Head, Wales.
	November 7th	LT270 *Reed*	Mined and sank in the Thames Estuary.
	November 12th	LT1141 *Lord Haldane*	Lost in the Bristol Channel, cause unknown. No contact since the 9th November. Part of her small boat was recovered on 15th November 1940 near Caldey Island by the trawler *J. A. P.*
	November 14th	LT1134 *Shipmates*	Sank following an air attack at Dover.
	November 14th	LT476 *The Boys*	Foundered during heavy weather whilst in The Downs, off South East England.
	November 18th	LT534 *Go Ahead*	Sank following a collision off Sheerness.
	December 5th	LT265 *Rendlesham*	Total loss after grounding on submerged rocks off Cape Clear Island, South West Ireland.
	December 17th	LT553 *Carry On*	Mined and sank off Sheerness.
	December 19th	LT747 *Proficient*	Total loss after grounding off Whitby.
	December 24th	LT212 *Lord Howard*	Sank after a collision in Dover harbour.
	December 26th	LT424 *True Accord*	Sank following a collision off Great Yarmouth.

Lowestoft Fishing Vessel Casualties 1939 - 1945 (Continued)

Date		Vessel	Cause of loss
1941	January 9th	LT895 *Dusky Queen*	Total loss after grounding in Dover Straits.
	February 3rd	LT585 *Midas*	Sank following a collision off Dungeness.
	February 10th	LT331 *Boy Alan*	Sank following a collision in the Thames Estuary.
	March 11th	LT123 *Aberdeen*	Sank after being attacked with gunfire and bombed by aircraft in Cardigan Bay, Wales.
	March 14th	LT90 *Peaceful Star*	Bombed and sank in the vicinity of Rockabill Lighthouse off the east coast of Ireland.
	March 29th	LT139 *Exeter*	Bombed and sank off Ballycotton on the south coast of Ireland.
	April 8th	LT317 *Hopton*	Mined and sank off Iceland.
	May 5th	LT187 *Fidelia*	Sank during an air attack on Lowestoft Harbour.
	May 8th	YH829 *Thistle*	Mined and sank off Lowestoft. (Lowestoft owned vessel)
	June 5th	LT1299 *Lavinia L.*	Sank off Sheerness after being bombed by enemy aircraft.
	June 13th	LT355 *King Henry*	Sank during an air attack on Lowestoft Harbour.
	July 1st	LT526 *Devon County*	Mined and sank in the Thames Estuary.
	July 7th	LT79 *Lord St. Vincent*	Mined and sank in the Thames Estuary.
	September 28th	LT269 *Murielle*	Mined and eventually sank off Blackpool.
	October 14th	LT1160 *Forerunner*	Sank following a collision in the Thames Estuary.
	November 25th	LT77 *Fisher Girl*	Sank during an air attack on Falmouth Harbour.
	December 8th	LT1151 *Bountiful*	Sank following a collision at Avonmouth.
1942	June 10th	LT1259 *Trusty Star*	Mined and sank off Malta.
	June 16th	LT240 *Justified*	Mined and sank off Malta.
1943	April 6th	LT706 *Golden Gift*	Sank following a collision with the ferry *Lochinvar* in Oban Bay. Wreck lies off Oban seafront in front of the Park Hotel.
1944	April 10th	LT223 *Forecast*	Sank at entrance to Albert Dock, Gourock after a collision.
	June 15th	LT293 *Gleam*	Sank following a collision.
	July 27th	LT153 *Rochester*	Mined and sank off the Yorkshire coast
1945	Nil		

Lowestoft Fishing Vessels Remembered - *Section One*

Some of the Casualties

LT230 *Ray of Hope*
Peter Killby Collection

LT57 *Eta*
Malcolm White Collection

LT265 *Rendlesham*
Malcolm White Collection

LT1141 *Lord Haldane*
Malcolm White Collection

Lowestoft Fishing Vessels Remembered - Section One

Some of the Casualties

YH65 *Fairbreeze*
Peter Killby Collection

LT79 *Lord St. Vincent*
Peter Killby Collection

LT355 *King Henry* (following an air attack)
Peter Killby Collection

LT90 *Peaceful Star*
Peter Killby Collection

Some of the Casualties

LT1299 *Lavinia L.*
Peter Killby Collection

LT895 *Dusky Queen*
Malcolm White Collection

LT1151 *Bountiful*
Malcolm White Collection

LT1259 *Trusty Star (as Elie Ness)*
Malcolm White Collection

Lowestoft Fishing and former Fishing Vessel Casualties 1946 - 1991

A selection of Lowestoft owned or registered vessels no longer in service due to reasons other than being life expired, scrapped, or being sold away from the port.

The fishing vessels listed include drifters, trawlers, a motorised smack and also former fishing vessels lost whilst being used as standby safety vessels to offshore structures and installations. Please note that this is a selection, and it is possible that there are other fishing and former fishing vessels lost between 1946 and 1991 which had associations with the port of Lowestoft.

The trawler LT313 *Sheriffmuir* was a well known member of the Lowestoft fleet for many years. However, she finished her working life as an Aberdeen registered standby safety vessel when on October 1st 1977 she grounded in thick fog near Murcar Golf Course whilst heading for Aberdeen. All the crew were taken off the vessel at low tide using a tractor and trailer. **Left** - A Sunday afternoon view of LT313 *Sheriffmuir* and other trawlers in the Waveney Dock during the 1950s. Built in 1952 at Hessle, *Sheriffmuir* was originally owned by the West Hartlepool Steam Navigation Co. Ltd. *Malcolm White Collection* **Right** - The standby safety vessel *Sheriffmuir* on the beach three miles north of Aberdeen. *Copyright James A. Pottinger*

Admiralty Standard Drifters and MFVs

In this section of the book the terms "standard" drifter and Motor Fishing Vessel (MFV) can be found describing some of the vessels. The following are explanations of these terms.

Admiralty "Standard" Drifters

A great many steam drifters were requisitioned by the Admiralty in World War One from individual owners and fishing companies for use in a variety of naval duties. In order to augment the number of drifters available from these sources a "standard" drifter design was produced by the Admiralty and it was intended that many of these would be built in various shipyards. Some of these "standard" drifters were of steel construction while others were built of wood. Several of the losses recorded in this book were "standard" drifters ordered by the Admiralty during World War One and completed during or immediately after that war.

Admiralty MFVs

A large number of wooden hulled diesel powered Admiralty Motor Fishing Vessels (MFVs) were built to standard designs during and immediately after World War Two for naval use, with the intention that they would be suitable for commercial purposes after becoming surplus to naval requirements. Following the end of World War Two many were released by the Admiralty and these were purchased by fishing companies and others for a variety of uses, including being adapted for use as pleasure craft.

Conversion of MFVs to fishing vessels was relatively easy and cost effective with the designs proving successful in their new roles that included trawlers, herring drifters and liners. They were constructed with different dimensions and of the trawler losses recorded in this book, two were of the 75ft. MFV class and the other two of the 90ft. MFV class.

Local Shipyards

To satisfy the Admiralty demand for "standard" drifters in World War One and MFVs in World War Two, numerous shipbuilders were involved in building these vessels including those in Oulton Broad and Lowestoft.

Top Right - A Royal Navy "standard" steam drifter at Lowestoft.
Centre Right - An example of a 75ft. MFV in naval service.
Bottom Right - An example of a 90ft. MFV in naval service.
All photographs from the Malcolm White Collection

****
Steam Drifter/Trawler SA116 *Lass O' Doune*
Sank in the English Channel in 1946 with no casualties

Not the *Lass O' Doune* but her identical sister ship BF251 *Loch Craig*
(At the present time no quality photograph is available of *Lass O' Doune*)
Courtesy Banffshire Maritime and Heritage Association

Vessel Details
Built - 1910
Shipbuilder - Hall, Russell & Co. Ltd., Aberdeen.
Official No. 127317
Call Sign - GWVC
Hull Construction - Steel
Dimensions (feet) - 86.1 x 18.6 x 9.0
Tonnage - 37.71nett / 91.24gross
Boiler Maker - Hall, Russell & Co. Ltd., Aberdeen
Engine Details - 41nhp Compound Steam Engine
Engine Builder - Hall, Russell & Co. Ltd., Aberdeen

Brief History

1910 Launched for Mr. George Falconer and others, Macduff, and registered as BF236.
1914 Sold to Mr. John J. George, Macduff.
1918 Hired by the Admiralty for naval duties in September at £55.12s.6d. per month.
1919 Returned to owner and resumed fishing as BF236.
1920 Sold to the Steam Pilot Boat (Cardiff and Bristol Channel) Co. Ltd., Pilotage Office, Cardiff and registered at Cardiff.
1940 In naval service as an examination vessel at Barry (Western Approaches Command, Cardiff Sub Command).
1940 Awarded £600 for salvage services rendered to Norwegian steamer *Hertha* which had been involved in a collision with a French steamer close to the *Breaksea* lightvessel. *Lass O'Doune* was on examination vessel duties close by at the time of the incident.
1942 Passed to Ministry of War Transport.
1943 Sold to Swansea owners and allocated fishing registration SA116.
1943 On October 14th the engine failed whilst fishing SSW of Ballycotton light. The trawler *Cyclamen* which was fishing nearby was requested to tow *Lass O' Doune* (estimated value £4,957) to Queenstown and Cork. *Cyclamen* was awarded £250 for towage and loss of fishing time.
1946 Mr. G. H. Claridge, White Cottage, Water End, Wheathampstead, purchased the vessel in February together with the steam drifter/trawler *Fertile* for £7000.
1946 Total loss after sinking off Shoreham.
2012 Wreck of the vessel located off Shoreham. United Kingdom Hydrographic Office reference No. 20120.

The loss of the *Lass O' Doune*

At the request of prospective purchaser Mr. G. D. Claridge, the *Lass O' Doune* was surveyed on September 11th 1945 with the result that it was found to be in need of considerable structural and mechanical repairs. A substantial number of important points were listed in the survey report including the number of wasted and patched shell plates, poor and holed bunker plates and repairs were needed to the engine and link motion. It was known that Mr. Claridge had wanted the steam drifter/trawler *Fertile,* but the owner would not sell that vessel without the *Lass O' Doune* being included in the sale. Mr. Claridge purchased the *Lass O' Doune* from Messers. Easton Brothers of Swansea for £3,000, and on October 4th 1946 she set sail from Newlyn for Lowestoft with a crew of six. The voyage to Lowestoft would be taken in stages and turned out to be beset with problems. On the first day the pumps, which proved to be consistently troublesome, were not capable of clearing the ingress of water into the vessel, and on the second day water was found in the stokehold. Because of her condition the *Lass O' Doune* made for Portland where the National Fire Service pumped her out. The next day she left Portland but returned to Weymouth where she was again pumped out. At Weymouth two members of the crew refused to sail and left the vessel and a third crew member, the cook, was dismissed. A gratuitous inspection of the engine room was carried out at Weymouth by local firm Messrs. Cousens but this was considered to be inadequate and not proper. The *Lass O' Doune* left Weymouth on October 8th 1946 but returned to Portland because of bad weather. She sailed from Weymouth in better weather but returned again due to her hull making water. She was again pumped out by shore labour. Arrangements were made for Lloyds Agent Mr. James Hamer to survey the drifter/trawler on October 9th, but the agent was told by the skipper, Mr. Reginald Rose, that the vessel was not making any water and his services were not required. The agent made no proper examination of the vessel and left. The *Lass O' Doune* left Weymouth on October 13th with a skipper, second hand, and two men of little trawler experience on board. At around teatime, the *Lass O' Doune* put into Southampton the reason being it was intended to sail only in daylight. On October 14th, she sailed at daybreak in fine weather from Southampton and again there was an ingress of water into the vessel due to various leaks. The situation worsened when before mid-day her pumps became choked and failed. At around 2.00pm, distress signals comprising "flag and shape" were exhibited on the vessel; her radio being out of order due to the batteries being run down. The *Lass O' Doune* was abandoned with her decks awash at around 5.00pm on October 14th 1946, the crew of four rowing to safety at Shoreham in the vessel's small boat. *Lass O' Doune* sank shortly afterwards and her remains together with her deck cargo of propellers were discovered by divers in 2012 off Shoreham. The Court of Inquiry into the loss of the vessel was held at The Temperance Institute, Carlton Crescent, Southampton on September 18th and 19th 1947 before R. F. Hayward Esq. K.C., assisted by Captain J. P. Thomson, Mr. J. Shand and Mr. J. Young. The Court considered that the vessel was undermanned since she had no competent engineer on board, and the skipper and the second hand had insufficient knowledge of her pumping arrangements. It also considered that it was wrong for the skipper to proceed with the voyage in view of the serious leaks, failure of the pumps and the refusal of some of the original crew to sail. It further considered that the skipper should have asked for the vessel to be drydocked either earlier at Weymouth or whilst at Southampton, but this was not done.

At the conclusion of the Court of Inquiry the official findings were that the loss of the vessel was due to her putting to sea with "unlocated leaks in her hull, with pumping arrangements in defective condition, and with an insufficient crew in that of the four men on board, none had sufficient knowledge of, and experience in, the use and maintenance of her pumping equipment."

The owner of the *Lass O' Doune*, Mr. Claridge asserted to the Court of Inquiry that the points raised in the September 1945 survey report had been taken up with the vendors who assured him that all the points raised in the report had been attended to during the last six months that they had owned the *Lass O' Doune*. However, some three months after purchasing the vessel, Mr. Claridge spent a total of £700 on essential repairs on her. It was made known to the Court that Mr. Claridge had been informed by his insurance brokers that it was essential for him to obtain a certificate of seaworthiness before leaving port.

The Court ordered Mr. Gordon David Claridge to pay £200 to the Ministry of Transport towards the cost of the Inquiry and also the drifter/trawler's skipper, Reginald Valentine Rose, to pay £250 to the Ministry of Transport towards the cost of the Inquiry.

Note
The drifter/trawler *Fertile* which was purchased by Mr. Claridge with the *Lass O' Doune* in 1946 was retired and sold for scrap in 1954, after eight years in the ownership of companies controlled by Mr. Claridge. Details and a photograph of the *Fertile* can be found in the book "Fishing with Diversity".

Hall, Russell & Co. Ltd. built many vessels similar to the *Lass O' Doune* two of which are seen here, PD145 *Jeannies* (Top) and PD149 *Peggy* (Bottom). No quality photograph of the *Lass O' Doune* is available at present.
Both photographs from the Malcolm White Collection

****
Steam Drifter/Trawler LT288 *Renascent*
Sprang a leak and sank in the North Sea in 1946 with no casualties

Left - Rigged for trawling, the wooden hulled *Renascent* heads out of Lowestoft in the 1930s.
Right - *Renascent* leaves Lowestoft for the herring fishing grounds.
Peter Killby Collection

Vessel Details
Built - 1926
Shipbuilder - Fellows & Co. Ltd., Southtown Dry Docks, Great Yarmouth
Official No. - 149192
Call Sign - GLLX
Construction - Wood
Dimensions (feet) - 85.7 x 19.7 x 10.2
Tonnage - 42.51nett / 100.47gross
Boiler Maker - Elliot & Garrood, Beccles
Engine Type - 230bhp "Admiralty" Triple Expansion Steam Engine
Engine Details - Cylinders (inches) - 9.5 & 15.5 & 26 x 18
Engine Builder - Elliot & Garrood, Beccles

Brief History

1926 Launched on April 14th by the wife of the owner, Mr. Stephen Granville Beamish. Vessel designed by Mr. H. Proctor and ship construction supervised by Mr. Alfred Castle.
1926 Sea trials commenced on May 26th and vessel registered on June 2nd as LT288.
1927 Top drifter at Yarmouth on October 3rd with 178 crans of herring.
1929 On December 10th towed into Lowestoft the sailing trawler *Leslie*, which had lost her main gaff and boom.
1932 Sold to Frederick William Moxey, "The Moorings", Gunton, Lowestoft on September 3rd.
1936 Provided assistance to steam drifter LT763 *Foresight* which was aground at Scarborough, helped in refloating the drifter.
1937 Sustained damage during a collision with the KY347 *Twinkling Star* in Yarmouth harbour on October 8th.
1938 Top drifter at Lowestoft on October 11th with 130 crans of herring.
1939 Requisitioned in November by the Admiralty for naval service as a minesweeper (Pennant No. FY.1520)
1941 Based at Sheerness.
1946 Returned to the owner in January.
1946 Registry closed at Lowestoft on September 16th after *Renascent* was sold to Norwegian owners for use as a trader.
1946 Sank in the North Sea on the way to her new owner.

The loss of the *Renascent*

With Skipper Christian Andreossen in charge, the *Renascent* left Lowestoft on Sunday October 27th 1946 with other local fishing vessels, but unlike the others which were engaged in the autumn herring fishing, she was bound for Kristiansand.
The vessel sprang a leak early on the morning of Monday October 28th approximate 70 miles from Lowestoft, the pumps were unable to clear the water entering *Renascent* and distress signals were hoisted which were seen by the steam trawler H224 *Grackle*, which was in the vicinity. Finding the *Renascent* was leaking too badly for towing, the crew of four were taken off by the *Grackle* and afterwards watched their vessel settle down in the water, and finally disappear. "It was fortunate we were in the locality" said one of the *Grackle's* crew, "because the weather was bad enough for our larger ship and the men would have had little chance in their small boat." Those rescued were Skipper Christian Andreossen; Magnus Larsen; Gunvold Tiorhon; and the engineer, Odd Olsen. Mr. Olsen lived in Bixley Place, Pakefield and was employed by the Lowestoft marine engineers L.B.S. Engineering Co. Ltd. He took the job on the *Renascent* as a way of getting to Norway where he intended having a holiday before returning home to Lowestoft. The local press reported that the crew of the *Renascent* were landed at Lowestoft on Tuesday October 29th by the *Grackle*.

Note
Although registered at Hull, the *Grackle* spent many years working out of Lowestoft and was considered a local trawler.

The steam trawler H224 *Grackle* rescued the crew of the *Renascent* and took them to Lowestoft. She is seen here about to enter Lowestoft on return from a fishing trip in August 1946.
Malcolm White Collection

****
Steam Drifter/Trawler LT1187 *S. D. J.*
Lost at sea with all her crew in 1947.

As a drifter, the *S. D. J.* makes for the pier heads at Lowestoft and the herring fishing grounds in the 1930s.
Malcolm White Collection

Vessel Details
Built - 1912
Ship builder - John Duthie Torry Shipbuilding Co. Ltd., Aberdeen.
Official No. - 132971
Call Sign - N/A
Construction - Steel
Dimensions (feet) - 87.3 x 18.45 x 9
Tonnage - 36.41nett / 99.86gross
Boiler Maker - Elliott & Garrood, Beccles
Engine Type - 25nhp Triple Expansion Steam Engine
Engine Details - Cylinders (inches) - 9.75 & 15 & 22 x 16
Engine Builder - Elliott & Garrood, Beccles

Brief History

1912 Built for Mr. James Smith (senior) of Lowestoft.

1912 Registered on August 28th as LT1187 S. D. J.

1915 Requisitioned in September for naval service as an anti-submarine net drifter. Allocated pennant No. 1857 and based at Dover where she became the flagship of the First Division of drifters on the Dover Patrol.

1919 Returned to owner.

1922 Owner died on August 17th and ownership of the vessel passed to Mr. James Smith (junior).

1937 Ownership of the vessel transferred to Mr. James Smith (junior) and Mr. Stephen Smith.

1939 Due to restrictions on North Sea fishing during the Second World War, the vessel fished from Fleetwood.

1947 Reported overdue since "on or about May 11th or 12th ".

1947 Lowestoft registry closed on June 4th.

The loss of the *S. D. J.*

The *S. D. J.* left Lowestoft on a fishing trip that was due to last one week and was expected to return to port on Monday May 12th 1947. In charge of the vessel was 39 year old Skipper Frank S. Church, who lived at 3 Higher Drive in Lowestoft. Other members of the crew, who were all from the Lowestoft area, were the Mate, Mr. W. Hart (54) of 17 Park Road; Third Hand Mr. A. E. Long (43) of 22 Cleveland Road; Chief Engineer Mr. W. Harman (64) of 97 Wollaston Road; Second Engineer Mr. A. Ames (50) of 15 Sandringham Road; Deck Hands Mr. L. C. Church (35) of 298 London Road South; Mr. C. F. Mobbs of 103 Ethel Cottages, Victoria Road; Mr. J. E. Winfield (29) of 14 Nelson Terrace, Pakefield and the Cook, Mr. R. J. Gooding of 20 Southwell Road. Deckhand Mr. L. C. Church was the brother of the skipper. The skipper was son-in-law of Mr. J. Smith of Peace Haven, Higher Drive, who with his son Mr. Stephen J. Smith, owned the *S. D. J.* Skipper Church had been married for ten years.

The last reported contact with the vessel was on Sunday May 11th 1947 when Skipper Church was heard on the radio discussing the weather and the progress of the trip with another skipper. Due to the expected return to port the following day, it was assumed that this radio call was made whilst the *S. D. J.* was heading home to Lowestoft and possibly not fishing at the time.

Nothing more was heard of the vessel until the arrival in Lowestoft on Thursday May 22nd of the steam drifter/trawler *Marshal Pak*. She reported that a damaged overturned small boat had been found belonging to the *S. D. J.*

A crew member of the *Marshal Pak* reported to an industry official "We had a feeling that we were going to find something and were keeping a especially sharp look out. First we saw a grating, such as our ships have outside the galley, and then we saw the small boat. It was upside down and had several holes in it as if heavy pieces of something had gone through it. When we righted the boat we found a lifebuoy belonging to the *S. D. J.* This was handed over to a fishery cruiser and we told them the position in which we had found the small boat".

On the following Saturday, further evidence to support the details given by the *Marshal Pak* crew member was revealed when the Lowestoft trawler *Warren* also reported having seen the small boat drifting 40 miles "outside" the Smith's Knoll light vessel as she was returning to port . The boat was no longer overturned having been righted by the crew of the *Marshal Pak* when they examined it. The Skipper of the *Warren* said the small boat from the *S. D. J.* had a big hole on one bow and that the bottom planking was loose.

The weather had been fine during the period of her disappearance and she had failed to make contact. These considerations plus the fact that the *S. D. J.* had not been seen for many days and had not returned to port when expected, led many people including those in the fishing industry to form the opinion that the vessel had sunk, probably as a result of an explosion caused by coming into contact with a wartime mine or similar explosive device. Hope of finding the *S. D. J.* was finally abandoned following the posting in official circles of reports of the items found by the *Marshal Pak* and the *Warren*.

Lowestoft Fishing Vessels Remembered - *Section Two*

No further evidence was forthcoming as to the fate of the *S. D. J.* and her crew, but it was thought that the end for the drifter/trawler and her crew of nine would probably have been swift. An industry official thanked the Skippers and the crews of the *Marshal Pak* and the *Warren* for their vigilance and help in understanding what had become of the *S. D. J.*

A memorial service for the crew of the missing vessel was held in Lowestoft in the chapel at the Mission to Seamen, where the Chaplain, the Rev. H. L. Newton Edwards, told the large congregation of the bravery of the crews of fishing vessels and went on to explain that "the harvest of the sea is gathered only at great risk", Skipper W. Thorpe read the Lesson and a collection was taken for the Lowestoft Fishermen's Widows and Orphans Fund.

A fund was set up by the Mayor, Mr. J. W. Woodrow, for the dependents of those lost on the *S. D. J.* In his letter to the local newspaper to launch the fund, the Mayor stated that he had just been made aware of the loss of another Lowestoft trawler, the *Bucentaur*, and her crew of ten.

The letter stated that the fund opened by the Mayor for the dependants of the *S. D. J.* would now embrace both trawlers. By early June 1947, the Mayor's *S. D. J.* and *Bucentaur* Distress Fund had reached £818. 3s.10d

The *S. D. J.* leaves Lowestoft on a fishing trip rigged for trawling.
Malcolm White Collection

The *Marshal Pak*, seen here leaving Lowestoft, found wreckage and the damaged upturned small boat from the *S. D. J.*
Photographer - Ernest Graystone
Copyright - Malcolm White

****
Steam Trawler LT170 *Bucentaur*
Lost at sea with her crew of ten following a collision in 1947

A scene full of memories at Lowestoft showing the *Bucentaur* about to enter the Waveney Dock and on the right, the drifter/trawler *Peaceful Star* passes through the pier heads for sea. In the foreground, four lads are fishing with hand lines.
Copyright Malcolm White

Vessel Details
Built - 1907
Shipbuilder - Cochrane & Sons, Selby. (Yard No. 420)
Official No. 125087
Call Sign - N/A
Construction - Steel
Dimensions (feet) -105 x 21.5 x 11.1
Tonnage - 88nett / 184gross
Boiler Maker - N/A
Engine Type - 57hp Triple Expansion Steam Engine
Engine Builder - Charles D. Holmes & Co. Ltd., Hull

Brief History

1907 Built for the Consolidated Steam Fishing & Ice Co. (Grimsby) Ltd. Grimsby and entered service as the steam trawler GY339 *Bucentaur*.
1914 Requisitioned by the Admiralty in August for naval use as a minesweeper.
1917 Returned to her owners in June.
1925 Transferred to Lowestoft in January and re-registered LT170.
1939 Requisitioned by the Admiralty in December for naval use as an auxiliary patrol vessel.
1940 Returned to the owner in January.
1947 Total loss in the North Sea following a collision.

Loss of the *Bucentaur*

On Tuesday May 20th 1947, the Consolidated Fisheries owned steam trawler *Bucentaur* left Lowestoft on a fishing trip expected to last 12 days. The last sighting of the *Bucentaur* was around midnight on May 20th - 21st from Skipper Challis on the trawler *Dereske* which reported that she and the *Bucentaur* were both heading for the Pit Buoy fishing grounds, about 148 miles from Lowestoft. Later a series of radio messages were received from the United States War Shipping Administration ship *Wilson Victory* concerning an incident. Due to dense fog the messages from the 7,600 ton vessel were not very specific with the first message, received at 1.16am G.M.T., stating that the steamer had been in collision with a small unknown craft two miles south west of a buoy off the Norfolk coast. After the earlier reports, the Baltimore registered *Wilson Victory* said "Vessel now stopped in this position in dense fog. Ships passing keep a sharp look-out for any shipwrecked person and drifting wreckage".

At 4.48am G.M.T. the American ship sent the following message: "Cancel urgency signal from *Wilson Victory*. The distress traffic is ended. Fog lifted at 1.54am. Made thorough search of the vicinity. Recovered lifeboat LT170. No persons observed. Cast lifeboat adrift and proceeding."

With the reported discovery of the small boat and no sign of the crew, suspicions immediately arose that the trawler LT170 *Bucentaur* was the other vessel involved in the collision. Attempts by the owners to obtain further information from the *Wilson Victory* had proved unsuccessful and repeated attempts to contact the trawler had failed to get any response.

However, the owners and the crew's relatives were still clinging to the hope that the ten missing men on the *Bucentaur* were safe. It was hoped that the trawler was still fishing but was having radio transmission problems preventing her making contact with other vessels or the coastal radio stations such as Humber Radio. All other vessels in the area had been asked to maintain a listening watch in case a message came through either from the *Bucentaur* herself or from a foreign port to which survivors had possibly been taken.

Nothing had been seen or heard of the *Bucentaur* since May 21st, 12 hours after she left Lowestoft, and the large American ship had seen little of the collision due to the fog but had found wreckage and the lifeboat. Later the sighting of substantial wreckage from the *Bucentaur* was reported by Skipper Albert Sandford of the Grimsby trawler *Exyahne* who testified that around 6.00am on May 21st, while about five miles west southwest from the Pit Buoy Light he saw a merchant ship circling a small lifeboat which had the port letters LT 170 horizontally across the stern. Nearby was a half circular life buoy also with the marking 'LT 170' on it, a pound board used for separating fish, a part of a bridge housing about ten or twelve feet square with what appeared to be the part where the trawler's bell would be. The bell support was later identified by the blacksmith who made it in Lowestoft as being from the *Bucentaur*. Some of the items recovered from the sea by the German trawler *Elbe* were passed to the Grimsby trawler *Marlborough* and landed at Grimsby. In addition to the wreckage found in the sea, part of the rigging from the *Bucentaur* was said to have been found on the port bow of the *Wilson Victory*.

On Wednesday June 4th, the families of the men who were on the *Bucentaur* were informed that the trawler must now be regarded as lost with all hands.

The crew of the *Bucentaur* were:- Skipper William James Besford (57), 68 Southwell Road, Lowestoft: mate, Frederick Jeremiah Warford (46), 168 The Avenue, Lowestoft: chief engineer, Harold D. Rose (47), Gladstone Cottages, Kessingland: second engineer, Benjamin A. Crowford (58), 35 Horn Hill, Lowestoft: third hand, Ernest G. Flowers (43), 73 Pakefield Street, Lowestoft: trimmers, Sam Durrant (26), 3, Hill Top, Kirkley Run, Lowestoft: Ronald J. Wheatley (18). 12 Edgar Road, Poplar: deckhands, Frederick W. Gowing (51), 15 Morton Road, Lowestoft, J. Sergeant (66), High Bank, London Road, Pakefield: cook, Michael Dann (66), Rhoda Cottages, Gisleham. The number lost would have been eleven but for the last minute transfer to another trawler of trainee deckhand D. P. Carr who lived at 112 Worthing Road, Lowestoft.

It was announced by the Mayor of Lowestoft within a few days of the *Bucentaur* disaster that the fund he had opened for the dependants of the crew of the missing drifter/trawler *S. D. J.*, would now be for the dependants of the crews of both vessels.

A memorial service to the ten men lost on the *Bucentaur* was held on Sunday June 8th 1947 at the Missions to Seamen Institute where the chapel was filled by relatives and friends of the crew, fishing industry representatives, civic leaders and representatives of the owners of the *Bucentaur*. The lesson was read by Skipper W. Thorpe of the RNMDSF. The trawler *Ostrich,* which belonged to the same company as the *Bucentaur,* left Lowestoft the following day carrying the floral tributes from the service. When she was at the location where the *Bucentaur* was hit and sank, the tributes were cast upon the sea.

It was reported a few years later in the media that two suits claiming a total of £287,500 had been filed in the United States by the dependants of the crew and also the owners of the *Bucentaur*. The dependant's suit was for £250,000 and the trawler's owner, Consolidated Fisheries Ltd., was for £37,500. Both suits were expected to be heard in 1954 at the United States Federal Court in San Francisco and in both cases the United States Government was the defendant. The charge was that the *Wilson Victory* was travelling at excessive speed in fog causing the death of all the crew of the trawler, and the loss of the vessel.

LT170 *Bucentaur* returning to her home port from a fishing trip.
Parry Watson Collection (2000)

LT107 *Ostrich* took the floral tributes to the position where the *Bucentaur* was lost. *Parry Watson Collection (2000)*

****

Steam Drifter LT89 *Present Friends*

Sprang a leak off Land's End in 1947 and later sank in Falmouth Bay with no casualties

Present Friends off the South Pier at Lowestoft in the 1920s.
Malcolm White Collection

Vessel Details
Built - 1914
Shipbuilder - S. Richards & Co. Ltd., Crown Works, Lowestoft (Yard No. 194)
Official No. - 136580
Call Sign - N/A
Construction - Wood
Dimensions (feet) - 86.6 x 19.2 x 9.3
Tonnage - 41.39nett / 89.04gross
Boiler Maker - Samuel Hodge & Sons Ltd., Millwall
Engine Type - 30nhp Compound Steam Engine
Engine Builder - S. Richards & Co. Ltd., Crown Works, Lowestoft

Brief History

1914 Ordered by William J. Turrell and Edmund T. Capps both of Lowestoft.
1914 Launched May 13th and registered on June 15th at Lowestoft. She ran sea trials on June 16th.
1915 Requisitioned in July by the Admiralty for use as anti-submarine net drifter. Allocated pennant No. 1565.
1916 Ownership transferred to Edmund Thomas Capps.
1918 On February 19th the *Present Friends* under Skipper Capps, the Lowestoft drifters *Lord Lovat, Accumulator, Placeo* and two other drifters, destroyed a German U-boat in mined nets 5miles south west of St. Catherine's Point, Isle of Wight.
1919 Vessel returned to the owner.
1927 Towed disabled LT585 *Midas* into Lerwick on June 23rd.
1927 Main steam pipe gave way in heavy weather on October 27th whilst off the Longships (Lands End). LT342 *Eileen Emma* stood by.
1929 Damaged in a collision with the steam drifter *Jasper* at Whalsay (Shetlands) on August 17th.
1929 Towed the damaged and disabled LT451 *Abiding Star* into Lowestoft on November 15th.
1937 Ownership transferred to E. T. Capps & Sons Ltd., Lowestoft.
1938 Damaged stem by striking the pier at Yarmouth on October 25th.
1939 Prunier Trophy winner with a catch of 194½ crans.
1940 Requisitioned in June by the Admiralty for naval duties and based in 1942 at Falmouth.
1946 Returned to the owner in October and Lowestoft registry closed. Sold to Claude Thomas Spriggs of Kessingland.
1947 In the ownership of D. Falster and others of Grimsby.
1953 Vessel at Shoreham awaiting disposal or breaking up.

The loss of the *Present Friends*

With ultimate intention of using the former drifter to go to Brazil and the Seven Seas, the *Present Friends* sailed from Lowestoft in June 1947. In August the drifter sprang a leak off Land's End whilst on passage between Littlehampton and Bristol and put into Helford where she was beached on a mudbank in the hope she would not sink. However, the *Present Fiends* slipped off the mudbank and foundered in Falmouth Bay. Six ex-servicemen were on board at the time and all escaped unhurt by getting off the partly submerged vessel in a dinghy. She was later refloated and taken to Falmouth where it was proposed to refit her. However the project seems to have been abandoned, and in 1953 the *Present Friends* was at a Shoreham shipbreakers yard apparently awaiting breaking up.

Right - *The Present Friends* partly submerged in Falmouth Bay. This image is from a report in a newspaper dated August 23rd 1948 which gives details of what the vessel was doing in Falmouth Bay and how those on board escaped from the sinking vessel.
Peter Killby Collection

****

Steam Drifter/Trawler KY232 *Plough*

Sank after striking a wreck in the English Channel in 1948. No casualties.

The Plough in Scottish waters as a drifter.
Malcolm White Collection

Vessel Details
Built - 1920
Shipbuilder - Isaac. J. Abdella & Mitchell, Queensferry. (Yard No. 445)
Official No. - 145552
Call Sign - GKND
Construction - Steel
Dimensions (feet) - 86.1 x 18.5 x 9.3
Tonnage - 39nett / 95gross
Boiler Maker - N/A
Engine Type - 42hp (270ihp) Triple Expansion Steam Engine
Engine Details - N/A
Engine Builder - Abdella & Mitchell, Queensferry.

Brief History

1920 Laid down for the Admiralty as a "standard drifter" and expected to become HMD *Foam*.
1920 Launched on October 1st.
1921 Not required by the Admiralty and completed as a fishing vessel. Transferred to the Fishery Board for Scotland on January 7th.
1921 Sold to J. & P. Thomson and others of Cockenzie, registered as LH288 and name changed to *Starwort*.
1923 Sold to M. & R. Gardner and others of Cellardyke
1923 Registered as KY232 and name changed to *Menat*.
1934 In the ownership of Mr. R. Gardner and renamed *Plough*
1938 Transferred to Mrs. Rachel F. Gardner, "Sunnyside", Williamson Street, Cellardyke.
1941 Requisitioned by the Admiralty for harbour service duties.
1942 Sold to North Shore Fishing Co. Ltd., Fleetwood.
1945 Returned to the owner.
1947 Trawling from Great Yarmouth.
1948 Vessel sank after coming into contact with a wreck in the English Channel.

The loss of the *Plough*

The Kirkcaldy registered *Plough* left Great Yarmouth on Friday April 9th 1948 for Fleetwood, with a view to working from that port. Her crew of nine were all Lowestoft men and the vessel was fishing for the Boston Deep Sea Fishing & Ice Company.

Near the East Goodwins she struck a wreck with the result that her keel was torn open and a mass of water entered her hull. This gave her crew barely enough time to get their belongings together, dress, and then launch and get into the vessel's small boat before she sank. The crew drifted helplessly for around four hours and burned clothing in the hope that it would attract attention. The next day (Saturday) the crew were picked up by the Ramsgate lifeboat. On reaching Ramsgate, all were given new clothing before being returned to their homes at Lowestoft.

The crew were: Skipper A. Spalding, 29 Stanford Street; Mate G. J. Clarke, 164 Raglan Street; Chief Engineer W. Clarke whose home was at Bradford; Third Hand R. G. Beamish, 18 Walmer Road; Second Engineer W. Turner, 57 Morton Road; Trimmer S. G. Moore, 15 Gorleston Road; Deck Hands J. Turrell, 88 Montgomery Avenue; R.C Shaw, 41 Newson's Meadow; and Cook F. W. Stevenson, 9 John Street.

The Chief Engineer who was below deck at the time the *Plough* collided with the submerged wreck said "When we hit the wreck it was like a thunder clap. Our ship shuddered and water began to pour in. When we were in the small boat and about 100yards away from the *Plough*, we saw her lights go out suddenly, and she slid down the side of the big ship which had sunk her."

Skipper Spalding stated "It all happened in a flash. We had no chance to collect our belongings. We launched our small boat and all nine of us crowded into it. We had only one oar and began to drift. Our hope was that the wind would not freshen."

Notes
North Shore Fishing Co. Ltd.
When the *Plough* sank she was owned by the North Shore Fishing Co. Ltd., which was a subsidiary company of the Boston Deep Fishing & Ice Company Ltd. This was one of a number of companies that operated trawlers out of Great Yarmouth during the post war period. Some of the vessels were large distant water vessels which at one time had operated out of the Humber ports.

****
Steam Drifter/Trawler LT98 *Mint*
Declared a total loss after grounding on a sandbank in Rosslare Bay in 1948. No casualties.

Rigged for drifting, the drifter/ trawler LT98 *Mint* is seen here with her second Buckie registration of BCK64. When advertised for sale on the sandbank where she grounded, *Mint* was described as a steam trawler.
Malcolm White Collection

Vessel Details
Built - 1912
Shipbuilder - Alexander Hall & Co. Ltd., Footdee, Aberdeen (Yard No. 479)
Official No. 132153
Call Sign - N/A
Hull Construction - Steel
Dimensions (feet) - 86.6 x 18.5 x 9.1
Tonnage - 41.36nett / 95.54gross
Boiler Maker - Alexander Hall & Co. Ltd.
Engine Type - 37nhp Triple Expansion Steam Engine
Engine Details - Cylinders (inches) - 9.25 & 16 & 26 x 18
Engine Builder - Alexander Hall & Co. Ltd.

Brief History

1912 Built for Mr. J. Reid and others, Buckpool, Buckie and registered as BCK125 *Mint*.
1915 Chartered from February 6th by the Admiralty for naval duties as a boom defence vessel at £59.1s.5d per month..
1919 Returned to the owners on July 11th.
1920 Sold to Offord & Geddes Ltd., Norwich and re-registered LT690 on March 22nd.
1923 Sold to W.H. East, Milford Haven.
1924 Sold to A. Coull, Buckpool, Buckie and re-registered BCK64 on March 26th.
1936 In the ownership of Catherine Coull & others, Buckpool, Buckie.
1941 Requisitioned by the Admiralty for use as a water carrier
1945 Returned to the owners.
1945 Sold to Messrs. Yolland Brothers and others, Milford Haven and re-registered at Lowestoft as LT98 on July 25th.
1948 In the ownership of the Cairo Fishing Co. Ltd., Milford Haven.
1948 Grounded on a sandbank off the Irish coast and eventually declared a total loss.
1948 Registry closed on November 19th.

The loss of the *Mint*

Whilst making for Rosslare in heavy weather on August 14th 1948, the *Mint* ran aground on a sandbank about four miles from Rosslare Pier. The crew were all rescued by the lifeboat *Duke of Connaught*, and the trawlers *Lord Anson* and *Cassiopeia* tried unsuccessfully to tow the *Mint* off the sandbank. Skipper G. E. Critten of 35 Shakespeare Avenue, Milford Haven stayed in Ireland for a few days after the grounding with the crew, to investigate various possibilities of refloating the vessel. The members of the crew were Mr. W. E. Bowen, Swansea: Mr. W. J. Musk, Manchester Square, Milford: Mr. M. McDonald, Greville Road, Milford: Mr. H. M. Evans, Llanelly: Mr. F. Male, 3 Main Street, Fishguard: Mr. W. Drake, 35 Edward Street, Milford and Mr. M. H. Thompson, 16 Greville Road, Milford. Efforts to refloat the vessel failed and she was offered by private tender to any interested party for breaking up "as she lies hard and fast on a sandbank". The disposal of the *Mint* was advertised in the "The Irish Times" of September 20th 1948 and it was hoped that the wreck would attract interest from scrap metal dealers. Skipper Critten later stated the *Mint* ran ashore since he was unable to see the lighted channel buoys owing to poor visibility and there being no readily available facilities for taking soundings.

Mint leaves port for the herring grounds. *Courtesy Ken Kent (1999)*

****
Steam Drifter LT172 *True Reward*
Sprang a leak and sank in the North Sea in 1948 with no casualties

A scene at Lerwick in the early 1920s showing English and Scottish drifters off the Esplanade, with True Reward in the centre.
Peter Killby Collection

Vessel Details
Built - 1913
Shipbuilder - S. Richards & Co. Ltd., Crown Works, Lowestoft (Yard No. 184)
Official No. - 135745
Call Sign - N/A
Construction - Wood
Dimensions (feet) - 85.9 x 19.8 x 9.55
Tonnage - 40.14nett / 92.96gross
Boiler Maker - Riley Bros., Stockton
Engine Type - 30nhp Compound Steam Engine
Engine Builder - S. Richards & Co. Ltd., Crown Works, Lowestoft

Brief History

1913 Built to the order of William Beamish, Charles E. Beamish and Isaac A. Beamish of Lowestoft, and registered on May 30th.
1915 Requisitioned in September by the Admiralty for use as a Boom Defence Vessel.
1919 Returned to owners.
1925 Ownership transferred to G. R. Beamish, Charles E. Beamish and Isaac A. Beamish.
1935 In collision with Fishery Protection Vessel HMS *Boyne* on October 16th whilst hauling her nets. Several planks stove in.
1940 Requisitioned by the Admiralty for use as a Mobile Wiping Unit. Allocated Pennant No. 1653 and based in 1942 at Liverpool.
1946 Returned to owners in February.
1946 Ownership transferred to Charles E. Beamish.
1948 Registry closed on September 2nd.
1948 Sold to Norwegian subjects for use as a trader.
1948 Sprang a leak and sank in the North Sea as she made her way to new owners in Norway.

The loss of the *True Reward*

The *True Reward* left Lowestoft for Norway on September 1st 1948 with Skipper B. Stensiand in charge and a Norwegian crew of four. However a few hours after leaving Lowestoft, the drifter sprang a leak and started to make considerable water whilst north east of the Smiths Knoll Light Vessel. The Lowestoft motorized smack *Try On* with Skipper Harry Saunders in charge was in the vicinity and took the Norwegians on board and then proceeded to tow the sinking drifter. She towed the stricken vessel for about four hours during which time the tow rope parted on two occasions in the difficult conditions. It was decided to abandon towing the *True Reward* since little headway was being made and the drifter, which was increasing likely to founder, was left unattended to the mercy of the sea.

Left - *True Reward* off the South Pier at Lowestoft in the 1920s. **Right** - The Lowestoft motor trawler and former sailing smack *Try On* provided assistance to the *True Reward* and her crew. *Both Photographs Peter Killby Collection*

Lowestoft Fishing Vessels Remembered - Section Two

****
Steam Drifter/Trawler LT593 *Golden Ring*
Foundered at sea in 1948 with no casualties.

Left - The *Golden Ring* leaves Lowestoft on a fishing trip rigged for trawling.
Right - Entering Lowestoft as a drifter but minus her fishing gear.
Malcolm White Collection

Vessel Details
Built - 1910
Shipbuilder - Cochrane & Sons Ltd., Selby.
Official No. - 129980
Call Sign - GSZT
Construction - Steel
Dimensions (feet) - 83.3 x 18.2 x 8.9
Tonnage - 34.91nett / 82.98gross
Boiler Maker - Riley Bros., Stockton
Engine Type - 32nhp Compound Steam Engine
Engine Builder - Crabtree & Co. Ltd., Southtown Ironworks, Southtown Road, Gt. Yarmouth

Brief History

1910 Launched for the Herring Fishing Co. Ltd., Lowestoft.
1910 Registered on June 26th.
1915 Requisitioned in September for naval service as an anti-submarine net drifter. Allocated Admiralty No. 1870 and based at Dover.
1919 Returned to owner.
1924 On March 23rd, Mr. George J. Gower, was lost overboard approximately 100miles NNE of the Hasbro' Light.
1931 On December 11th, Mr. Stanley Sabberton was lost overboard off the French Coast.
1936 Sold to Ritson J. Tripp, The Beeches, Kessingland.
1944 Ownership of the vessel transferred to Carry On Fishing Co. Ltd., Lowestoft.
1948 Vessel sank at sea after she sprang a leak in heavy weather.
1948 Registry closed on November 9th.

Note - There was another steam drifter/trawler named *Golden Ring* owned by the same company at Lowestoft. This worked from the port from 1952-1957 and a photograph of that vessel can be found in the book "Herrings, Drifters and the Prunier Trophy".

The loss of the *Golden Ring*

The *Golden Ring* sprang a leak and foundered whilst herring fishing 27 miles ESE of Lowestoft on October 30th 1948. All the crew were rescued by the drifter/trawler LT180 *Playmates* which was in the vicinity. In addition to the *Playmates* assisting with the rescue, the motor trawler *Sunlit Waters* was also in attendance and did attempt to tow the *Golden Ring* while it seemed possible that she might remain afloat.

The *Playmates* saved the crew of the *Golden Ring* and took them back to Lowestoft.
Displaying her original registration of YH141, she is seen here about to enter
Lowestoft harbour in the 1930s on return from the herring grounds.
Malcolm White Collection

****
Steam Trawler LT308 *Mary Heeley*
Total loss after grounding on rocks to the north of Douglas Bay in 1950 with no casualties.

The *Mary Heeley* as the Royal National Mission to Deep Sea Fishermen's
mission ship/trawler LO197 *Sir Edward P. Wills*. She is seen here leaving Lowestoft.
Malcolm White Collection

Vessel Details
Built - 1937
Shipbuilder - Goole Shipbuilding & Repairing Co Ltd., Goole
Official No. 165441
Call Sign - GZMJ
Construction - Steel
Dimensions (feet) - 101.2 x 21.2 x 10.3
Tonnage - 60nett / 162gross
Engine Type - 41hp Triple Expansion Steam Engine
Engine Builder - Crabtree (1931) Ltd., Southtown Ironworks, Southtown Road, Great Yarmouth

Brief History

1937 Built for the Royal National Mission to Deep Sea Fishermen, 68 Victoria Street, London S.W.1. and entered service as the Mission ship/side trawler LO197 *Sir Edward P. Wills*.
1939 Requisitioned in September for naval service as an examination vessel at Great Yarmouth.
1945 Returned to her owner in August.
1947 Sold to Small & Co. (Lowestoft) Ltd. subsidiary Vigilant Fishing Co. Ltd. in August and re-registered LT308 in October.
1947 Shaft on winch broke in October.
1948 In service as LT308 *Mary Heeley*.
1949 Propeller fouled by nets at Milford Haven in March.
1949 Propeller damaged by trawl door in June.
1950 Total loss after grounding on rocks off the Isle of Man.

Loss of the *Mary Heeley*

On April 29th 1950, the Lowestoft steam trawler *Mary Heeley* put into Douglas in the Isle of Man to seek medical help for a crew member. In foggy conditions she left Douglas shortly before midnight and after leaving port hit rocks off Onchan and grounded. She sounded an S.O.S. on her steam horn which was heard by those on shore who contacted the harbour master at Douglas. The lifeboat was launched and proceeded to the stricken trawler where she rescued the trawler's crew of ten. The weather during the next two days was bad with the result that the *Mary Heeley* was driven further on to the rocks and in the process her hull was severely damaged as was her propeller. In addition, the top section of her wheelhouse and small boat were swept away. The former mission ship was declared a total loss and abandoned at her last resting place at Bank's Howe, where apparently her remains are still visible under certain conditions

The Lowestoft trawler *Mary Heeley* wrecked near Douglas in the Isle of Man.
Courtesy - Small & Co. (Lowestoft) Ltd.

****
Motor Fishing Vessel LT232 *Aylesby*
Caught fire, abandoned and sank in the North Sea in 1951 with no casualties.

The Aldred Fishing Co. Ltd. owned *Aylesby* at Grimsby before she joined
the Lowestoft fleet in 1951, and her demise the same year.
Malcolm White Collection

Vessel Details
Built - 1946
Shipbuilder - East Anglian Constructors Ltd., Oulton Broad (Yard No. 364)
Official No. - 166649
Call Sign - MBDL
Construction - Wood
Dimensions (feet) - 92.4 x 22.25 x 9.8
Tonnage - 41.39nett / 111.89gross
Engine Type - 4 cylinder 240 hp Diesel
Engine Builder - Crossley Bros. Ltd., Openshaw, Manchester.

Brief History

1946 Ordered in July 1944 and intended to be the standard wartime Admiralty Motor Fishing Vessel MFV1579, but the order was cancelled and the shipbuilder sought prospective purchasers for the uncompleted vessel.
1946 Sold to Aldred Fishing Co. Ltd., Grimsby.
1946 Converted for use as a trawler by Shire Trawlers Ltd. and Humphrey & Smith Ltd., Grimsby.
1946 Registered as GY329 *Aylesby*
1951 Sold to Huxley Fishing Co. Ltd., Lowestoft and re-registered as LT232.
1951 Vessel sank in the North Sea after catching fire.

The loss of the *Aylesby*

"She was an awful sight, blazing from stem to stern, flames and smoke belching up to the top of the mast and the sea boiling and hissing around her. I never want to see the likes again," was how Skipper Joe Cook, whose home was at 3 Elm Tree Road, described the final scene at 3.00am on Wednesday May 9th 1951, as the Lowestoft trawler *Aylesby* sank after burning for around 24hours. Skipper Cook was speaking to a local newspaper reporter in the cabin of the steam trawler H852 *Isle of Wight*, which went alongside the burning vessel, and rescued the skipper and his crew. Skipper Cook said the fire started after the drive belt of the winch caught fire and fell amongst the engines. At once there was a mass of flames and the crew started to tackle the fire with extinguishers. "We battened and sealed down the whole ship, doors, ventilators and everything so that no draught could get down to the fire," he continued. "I told the crew to get the small boat out and then I got on my wireless but when one of the small diesel tanks blew up, my receiving set was put out of action. Fortunately I was able to continue sending out messages."

"Beyond question" continued Skipper Cook, "our wireless saved us. The nearest ship to us when we caught fire, 70 miles north-east by north of Smith's Knoll, was the *Isle of Wight* and she was 30 miles away. While I was able to send on my wireless I got in touch with another trawler which was at that time 50 miles away and she told the *Isle of Wight* of our plight and directed her to us."

Skipper Cook said he kept the small boat in readiness, but there was a lot of sea and wind and the boat was half filled with water and one of the crew volunteered to go down and bail her out. "There were still heavy seas and a lot of wind when the *Isle of Wight* got to us," Skipper Cook went on "and when we decided to abandon the *Aylesby* it was risky to use the boat which it had been discovered, had a plank stove in. After three attempts Skipper Charles Honeywood skilfully brought the *Isle of Wight* alongside and we had to jump for it."

Note
Although registered at Hull, the *Isle of Wight* spent many years working out of Lowestoft and was considered a local trawler.

The steam trawler *Isle of Wight* which, under Skipper Honeywood, rescued the crew of the *Aylesby*. The *Isle of Wight* is seen here in August 14th 1949 approaching the harbour entrance at Lowestoft
Malcolm White Collection

****

Motor Trawler LT1224 *Flag Jack*

Beached to prevent her sinking after reversing into the South Pier in 1952 with no casualties.

Flag Jack was fitted with a stern wheelhouse in 1924 and following her later conversion to full motor power was provided with a different wheelhouse further forward. This small motor trawler is seen from the South Pier at Lowestoft entering the harbour.
Malcolm White Collection

Vessel Details
Built - 1921
Shipbuilder - Colby Bros. Ltd., Oulton Broad
Official No. - 145771
Call Sign - GRRP
Construction - Wood
Dimensions (feet) - 72.0 x 18.9 x 9.1
Tonnage - 35.9nett / 65.13gross
Engine Type - 3cylinder 100hp Diesel
Engine Builder - Deutz AG, Cologne, Germany

Brief History

1921 Built for Frederick Chapman and registered on March 17th 1921 as the sailing trawler LT1224 *Flag Jack*.
1921 Sold to Reginald. C. Colby, Lowestoft.
1924 Fitted with an auxiliary engine and a wheelhouse, but retained her full set of sails.
1926 Sold to Lowestoft Fish Selling Co. Ltd., Herring Market, Lowestoft.
1927 Sold to Herbert I. Podd, Lowestoft.
1928 Ownership transferred to W. H Podd Ltd., Trawl Market, Lowestoft.
1930 Fitted with 100hp diesel engine.
1933 During September grounded and was holed off Lowestoft on one of the sandbanks. The engine was put out of order due to waterlogging of the vessel. She was towed off and beached in the harbour.
1941 In service with the Admiralty as an Examination Service Vessel at Brixham.
1941 Sent out in gale force winds on April 1st to retrieve a small boat which was adrift from a Royal Navy vessel.
1945 Sold to A. E. Dexter, Brixham
1947 In the ownership of Fleetwood Drifters Ltd., Paignton.
1952 Following an explosion on board, reversed into the South Pier causing damage to the stern. She was beached to prevent her sinking.
1953 Broken up.

The loss of the *Flag Jack*

Following a six months refit, the *Flag Jack* was set to carry out sea trials in Lowestoft Roads on the December 9th when trouble was experienced with the engine. Engineer Mr. Jack Fakes of Police Station Road, Lowestoft recalled: "When we were about a mile out of the harbour entrance smoke started to come from the engine. I told my skipper, Mr. William Reynolds, who reduced speed and we turned back into harbour. We had completely stopped when there was an explosion. The engine just blew up and flames shot up into my face. However, *Flag Jack* must have put herself into gear by her own internal gasses, for she started to go astern".

Mr. Fakes continued: "Meanwhile, I had managed to put out the fire with the extinguishers we always have on board. However, with the stern smashing into the pier we had to start getting out our gear, and members of the crew got out and scrambled on to the pier, being given assistance by anglers and others. The tug *Lowestoft* then came alongside and took *Flag Jack* in tow. Three of us went back on board off the pier and the tug managed to get *Flag Jack* into the Waveney Dock where she was beached. She had started to take water since she collided with the pier". Skipper Reynolds of 13 Sussex Road, Lowestoft said he was anxious to thank everybody who had helped from the pier at the critical time when the vessel collided with it. He continued: "The force of the explosion nearly threw me off the bridge. The force of it seemed to throw the engine full astern, for we went full speed into the stone piers, stoving in our stern". The three members of the crew who returned to the vessel were Mr. Fakes, the mate Mr. Jack Fisher and Mr. George Gilby, the third hand. The *Flag Jack* was later refloated by the British Railways vessels *Mudsucker*, *Pioneer* and *Progress* but was further damaged in the salvage operation. She was broken up in 1953.

The *Flag Jack* beached on the east side of the Waveney Dock.
Peter Killby Collection

Lowestoft Fishing Vessels Remembered - *Section Two*

****

Motor Trawler LT73 *Guava*
Lost at sea with her entire crew in 1953.

The Guava heading out of Lowestoft for the fishing grounds.
Malcolm White Collection

Vessel Details (as in 1951)
Built - 1943/44
Shipbuilder - Messrs. Peter Hancock and Sons, Pembroke Dock
Official No. 166722
Call Sign - GDNL
Construction - Composite
Dimensions (feet) - 140 x 26 x 12
Tonnage - 106nett / 285gross
Engine Type - 6 cylinder 540hp diesel
Engine Builder - National Gas and Oil Engine Co. Ltd., Ashton-under-Lyne

Brief History

1943 Launched as motor minesweeper MMS 1039 for the Royal Navy.
1944 Commissioned on September 26th.
1946 Transferred to the French Navy and given the pennant number D341.
1948 Purchased by Mr. G. H. Claridge, White Cottage, Water End, Wheathampstead
1948 The minesweeper arrived at Lowestoft for conversion by marine engineers William Overy & Sons into what was to become at that time, the largest trawler to work from the port.
1949 Ownership transferred to Claridge Trawlers Ltd., Lowestoft.
1953 Contact lost on the night of the great storm of January 31st, whilst on a herring fishing trip in the southern North Sea.

The loss of the *Guava*

The *Guava* left Lowestoft on Friday January 30th 1953 under Skipper George (Tosh) Fisher and headed south for the Sandettie fishing grounds to trawl for herring. On the night of the great storm, January 31st 1953, Skipper Fisher spoke on the radio to his wife at 7.15pm and later to a skipper, also at sea in the storm aboard the Lowestoft trawler *Ala*. Skipper Harold Soanes, a friend of Skipper Fisher, received a call at 7.20pm and also at 10.00pm, in both calls Skipper Fisher indicated that the sea was very bad and that was he was "dodging" and wished he was off Southwold, where the *Ala* was sheltering from the storm. Skipper Fisher said he would call the *Ala* the next morning at 8.15am but nothing was heard. The Skipper of the *Ala* called the *Guava* several times during the day but received no reply. Skipper Soanes stated at the Court of Inquiry into the loss of the *Guava* that Skipper Fisher had previous told him that the *Guava* was the finest sea ship he had ever sailed in. After being asked what he thought had happened to the *Guava*, Skipper Soanes went on to say that in his opinion the *Guava* capsized and that it happened very quickly.

The Court heard from a report issued by the Meteorological Office that on the night of January 31st - February 1st 1953, the weather conditions experienced in the area where the trawler and her crew were lost were "extremely severe and almost unprecedented" with gusts up to force 12 being experienced. Meteorological Office representative Mr. Robert Haigh stated that it had been estimated that there were waves of 28 feet at midnight on January 31st rising to 30 feet by 4.00am on 1st February in the area the *Guava* was expected to have been in.

Details of those lost on the *Guava*
George Fisher, Skipper, aged 41
Roy Dann, mate, aged 32
Henry Taylor, chief engineer, aged 38
Robert Girling, engineer, aged 45
Arthur Howe, third hand, aged 58
Louis George Chapman, deck hand, aged 42
G. H. Stone, engineer, 34
George Turner, deck hand, aged 58
Edward Sizer, deck hand, aged 38
Anthony Folkard, deckie learner, aged 16
J. H. Vince, cook, aged 40

16 year old Anthony Folkard was making his first trip as a deckie learner on the *Guava*.

The Court of Inquiry into the loss of the *Guava* was held over three days in the ballroom of the Royal Hotel in November 1953 with 22 witnesses being called, some of whom having had first hand experience of sailing on the *Guava*. One of these, Mr. Albert Lockwood, had been mate on the trawler for two years and said off the Norwegian coast the *Guava* behaved well in a "bad breeze". Another past crew member, second engineer Mr. Frederick Cable, stated that the *Guava* could cross the Atlantic and that he had never been afraid of the safety of the ship in the nine months he sailed on her. A skipper who had been in charge of the *Guava* for over three years, stated that she was the best sea boat he had sailed on. The findings of the Court were that it was unable to definitely say what caused the trawler to sink with all its eleven crew and without leaving any trace, but it did find that "the probable cause was the sudden overwhelming of the vessel by the force of the wind and the high confused state of the sea".

A memorial service to the crew of the *Guava* was held at the Seamen's and Fisherman's Bethel on Sunday 8th March 1953. The chapel was full with many of those attending having to stand for the service which was conducted by the port missionary of the British Sailors Society, Mr. Harry Kirby, assisted by Skipper E. Goldspink of the Royal National Mission to Deep Sea Fishermen.

Amongst the civic leaders attending were the Mayor and Mayoress (Mr. and Mrs. W. H. B. Sanders), the Deputy Mayor and Mayoress (Mr. And Mrs. H. J. Stebbings) and the Town Clerk (Mr. F. B. Nunney). Representatives of the fishing industry included Mr. G. D. Claridge (chairman of Claridge Trawlers [owners of the *Guava*]) and Mrs. Claridge, Mr. D. A. Stephens (manager of Claridge Trawlers), Mr. A. W. Suddaby (chairman of the Lowestoft Fishing Vessels Owners Association) and Mr. F. E. Catchpole (chairman of the English Herring Catchers Association). A collection, which amounted to £33.15s., was taken for the Mayor's *Guava* Fund.

Note
Guava was originally one of the MMS 1001 series of minesweepers of which over 100 were built. These vessels served with several navies including the Royal Norwegian Navy, Royal Dutch Navy, Soviet Navy and the Royal Navy. The majority were built in U.K. shipyards with others being built in Canada. A photograph of a newly completed MMS 1001 series minesweeper can be found on the next page. The *Guava* was not the only former MMS 1001 series minesweeper to serve as a trawler after becoming surplus to naval requirements.

MEMORIAL SERVICE
TO THE
SKIPPER AND CREW
OF THE

"GUAVA"

PRESUMED LOST AT SEA 31st JANUARY, 1953

HELD IN

LOWESTOFT SAILORS' AND FISHERMEN'S
BETHEL
BATTERY GREEN ROAD

SUNDAY, 8TH MARCH, 1953
AT 6-30 p.m.

GEORGE FISHER, *Skipper.*

ROY DANN, *Mate.*   HENRY TAYLOR, *Chief Engineer.*
G. H. STONE, *Engineer.*   ROBERT GIRLING, *Engineer.*
ARTHUR HOWE, *3rd Hand.*   GEORGE CHAPMAN, *Deck Hand.*
GEORGE TURNER, *Deck Hand.* EDWARD SIZER, *Deck Hand.*
ANTHONY FOLKARD, *Decky Learner.* J. H. VINCE, *Cook.*

In attendance with the families of the above-named
HIS WORSHIP THE MAYOR OF LOWESTOFT,
COUNCILLOR W. H. B. SANDERS, J.P.,
AND MEMBERS OF THE BOROUGH COUNCIL.

The front cover of the Order of Service used at the Bethel on Sunday March 8th 1953.
(Reduced in size for inclusion in this book)
Malcolm White Collection.

Lowestoft Fishing Vessels Remembered - *Section Two*

Top - A newly completed example of the type of Royal Navy vessel the *Guava* was when she entered service in 1944 as MMS *1039*. This vessel was one of several minesweepers that were built at Lowestoft and Oulton Broad and is seen here waiting to pass through the town's swing bridge.
Malcolm White Collection

Centre - A view from the South Pier of *Guava* as she is about to enter Lowestoft harbour after a fishing trip.
Malcolm White Collection

Bottom - *Guava* in the Outer Harbour at Lowestoft and heading for sea.
Malcolm White Collection

****
Steam Drifter/Trawler LT273 *Lord Duncan*
Sank at Lowestoft North Quay in 1954 with no casualties.

A few years before she was sold for scrap in 1954 following her sinking, the Lord Duncan enters the Waveney Dock at Lowestoft during an autumn herring fishing season.
Malcolm White Collection

Vessel Details
Built - 1920
Shipbuilder - Kings Lynn Shipbuilding Co. Ltd., Kings Lynn.
Official No. - 144801
Call Sign - GKNL
Construction - Steel
Dimensions (feet) - 86.9 x 18.55 x 9.3
Tonnage - 41.23nett / 97.15gross
Boiler Maker - A. Dodman & Co. Ltd., Kings Lynn
Engine Type - 42nhp Triple Expansion Steam Engine
Engine Details - Cylinders (inches) - 9.5 & 15.5 & 26 x 18
Engine Builder - A. Dodman & Co. Ltd., Kings Lynn

Brief History

1920 Laid down for the Admiralty as a "standard drifter" and expected to become HMD *Melody* (Admiralty No. 4172).
1921 Completed as a fishing vessel and transferred to the Fishery Board for Scotland on February 4th.
1921 Sold to J. Duthie and A. Fyfe, Aberdeen.
1921 Entered commercial service as the drifter/trawler A666 *Rose Duncan*.
1922 Sold to James Murray Snr., Buckie and re-registered at Buckie as BCK122.
1937 Sold to Joseph Catchpole, Scarborough, George Scotter, Filey, and William Sayer, Filey.
1937 Vessel re-registered at Scarborough as SH105.
1947 Sold to Lowestoft Herring Drifter Co. Ltd.
1947 Vessel re-registered at Lowestoft as LT273 on January 8th.
1949 On May 15th the *Rose Duncan* was renamed *Lord Duncan*.
1954 *Lord Duncan* sank at North Quay, Lowestoft; she was raised and later sold for scrap.

The loss of the *Lord Duncan*

The *Lord Duncan* sank in the early hours of Wednesday July 7th at North Quay, Lowestoft after being coaled from a railway truck the previous day. She was rigged for trawling and being prepared for her next fishing trip. It was stated at the time by a representative of her owners that they believed she somehow got caught under the quay heading on the overnight rising tide and started to take on water and finally sank. The drifter/trawler was raised after divers had sealed off her hatches and bunkers during the afternoon of July 7th. She was then laid up for several weeks while her fate was being decided. The decision of the owners was to scrap the vessel and consequently all usable items and any gear suitable for further use were removed from her. *Lord Duncan* left Lowestoft on October 27th in tow of the steam trawler *Ouse* bound for Antwerp, where both vessels were scrapped.

An image from a newspaper report of the *Lord Duncan* after she sank at the North Quay on July 7th 1954.
Peter Killby Collection

After being made seaworthy for the crossing of the North Sea, the *Lord Duncan* leaves Lowestoft in tow of the trawler *Ouse* for a shipbreakers yard in Belgium. *Peter Killby Collection*

****

Motor Drifter/Trawler LT166 *Gypsy Queen*

Lost at sea with her entire crew in 1955.

The Gypsy Queen leaving Lowestoft on a fishing trip. At the time of her loss she was still considered a comparatively new vessel.
Malcolm White Collection

Vessel Details

Built - 1950
Shipbuilder - Henry Scarr Ltd., Hessle
Note - The Henry Scarr shipyard was acquired in 1932 by Richard Dunston Ltd. but shipbuilding at the Hessle yard continued under the Henry Scarr name until the early 1960s.
Official No. 183963
Call Sign - GKFQ
Construction - Steel
Dimensions (feet) - 84.5 x 21.6 x 8.9
Tonnage - 82.45nett / 113.63gross
Engine Type - 6cylinder 360hp Diesel.
Engine Builder - Mirrlees, Bickerton & Day, Stockport.

Brief History

1950 Built for the West Hartlepool Steam Navigation Co. Ltd., West Hartlepool and entered service as the side trawler LT166 *Gypsy Queen* however, she was launched as the *Gitana*.
1950 Registered on June 3rd and commenced working out of Lowestoft.
1955 Presumed lost with her Skipper and crew approximately 80 miles north west of Heligoland in a severe gale.

Loss of the *Gypsy Queen*

The *Gypsy Queen*, under Skipper Gordon Smith, left Lowestoft on the evening of Monday January 10th 1955 and since Wednesday January 12th, no radio calls or sightings had been received.

A severe gale occurred on the Wednesday night in the area where the *Gypsy Queen* was thought to have been. On Thursday January 13th, Skipper Charles Honeywood of the Lowestoft trawler *Ludham Queen* sent the following radio message: "At about 8.30am G.M.T. passed an overturned ship, may be fishing vessel about 90ft. long". Some of the crew of the *Ludham Queen* commented that it was an all welded vessel but it was so low in the water that positive identification was impossible. Later on Thursday, a message from Reuters at the Hook of Holland stated "Several ships and a Dutch air-sea rescue craft failed to find possible survivors from an upturned vessel about 90 feet long spotted by the Lowestoft trawler *Ludham Queen* about 60 miles east of Denmark this morning".

Later on Thursday, the German trawler *Klaus Mollerdhig* sent a message stating she was at the "wreck position" and added: "There are several ships searching for the ship but nothing found yet".

As radio contact with the *Gypsy Queen* could not be established and no ship had reported seeing the trawler, a general broadcast for ships to be on the look out for her was transmitted on Monday January 17th. Around midnight on Monday, the Grimsby trawler *Strephon* reported to Humber Radio that she saw a damaged lifeboat or small boat with the *Gypsy Queen*'s markings of LT166 last Thursday, about 10 miles from the reported position of the upturned ship. The boat was partially submerged.

With rumours circulating in Lowestoft about the fate of the *Gypsy Queen*, Mr. Suddaby, representing the owners, and Mr. J. Kirby, Lowestoft Port Missionary, visited relatives of the crew and told them of their anxiety for the safety of the vessel.

The *Ludham Queen* arrived back at Lowestoft late on Wednesday January 19th and after interviewing Skipper Honeywood and the crew, Mr. Suddaby issued the following statement to the press:

"Skipper Honeywood has told me that on the morning of Thursday January 13th, he came past in very bad weather an upturned hull of what appeared to be a fishing vessel. Owing to the bad weather conditions he could not get very close to it and he thought at the time it was a German fishing vessel of which several were known to be fishing in the locality. He reported this to Norddeich Radio at 8.30am and during the day when the weather had moderated slightly, he returned to the position where he had seen the upturned hull. By this time an aircraft was flying over the locality and directed him to the position of the capsized vessel. This time he got close enough to see it was a welded steel hull and only the stern was showing, but occasionally, with the rise of water they saw a white band similar to the markings of the *Gypsy Queen*, and also one of the crew thought he saw the last figure of the vessel's number which appeared to be a figure six. This would correspond with the last figure of the *Gypsy Queen*'s number".

Mr. Suddaby continued: "After hearing this, coupled with the sighting of the lifeboat by the Grimsby trawler *Strephon*, I have with the greatest regret come to the conclusion that the upturned vessel could be none other than the *Gypsy Queen*". He assumed the trawler had been lost in the storm during the night of Wednesday January 12th and he was reporting her as missing to the Ministry of Transport.

The skipper of the *Gypsy Queen* was 49 year old Gordon Smith who lived at 27 Florence Road, Pakefield. Since the Second World War, he had only been to sea on fishing vessels owned or managed by the Boston Deep Sea Fishing & Ice Co. Ltd.

The trawler's crew were:
Mate	Mr. W. Beamish, 2 Belvoir Cottages, Carlton Colville
Third Hand	Mr. R. G. Beamish, 5 Westwood Avenue, Whitton Estate, Lowestoft
Chief Engineer	Mr. E. Baldry, 22 Oakwood Road, Whitton Estate, Lowestoft
Deck Engineer	Mr. F. Last, 30 Arnold Street, Lowestoft
Cook	Mr. A. Wigg, 115 Victoria Road, Oulton Broad
Deckhand	Mr. J. W. Rising, 7 Priory Street, Gorleston.

For Mr. R. G. Beamish, who was not related to Mr. W. Beamish, this was his first fishing trip on the *Gypsy Queen*.

The skipper and crew of the Lowestoft trawler *Ludham Queen* **(above)** saw an upturned hull which was probably that of the *Gypsy Queen*.
Malcolm White Collection

MEMORIAL SERVICE

TO THE

SKIPPER AND CREW

OF THE

"GYPSY QUEEN"

PRESUMED LOST AT SEA 12th JANUARY 1955

HELD IN

LOWESTOFT SAILORS' AND FISHERMEN'S BETHEL

BATTERY GREEN ROAD.

SUNDAY, 6th FEBRUARY, 1955

at 6-30 p.m.

———

Gordon Smith, *Skipper.*

W. G. Beamish, *Mate.* E. W. Baldry, *Chief Engineer.*
R. G. Beamish, *Third Hand.* F. Last, *Deck Engineer.*
A. A. Wigg, *Cook.* J. W. Rising, *Deck Hand.*

———

In attendance with the families of the above-named.

His Worship The Mayor of Lowestoft,
Alderman J. M. Lang, J.P.,
and Members of the Borough Council.

A memorial service to the skipper and crew of the *Gypsy Queen* was held on Sunday February 6th 1955. The front cover of the Order of Service is shown above, this has been reduced in size for inclusion in this book
Malcolm White Collection

Lowestoft Fishing Vessels Remembered - *Section Two*

****
Steam Drifter/Trawler LT180 *Playmates*
Lost at sea with her entire crew in 1955.

Playmates approaching the pier heads at Lowestoft on return from a fishing trip.
Malcolm White Collection

Vessel Details
Built - 1925
Shipbuilder - Cochrane & Sons Ltd., Selby. (Yard No. 964)
Official No. 144146
Call Sign - GYGQ
Construction - Steel
Dimensions (feet) - 86.3 x 18.6 x 9
Tonnage - 41.36nett / 92.7gross
Boiler Maker - Riley Bros., Stockton
Engine Type - 27nhp Triple Expansion Steam Engine
Engine Details - Cylinders (inches) - 9 & 14.5 & 23 x 16
Engine Builder - Crabtree & Co. Ltd., Southtown Ironworks, Southtown Road, Gt. Yarmouth

Brief History

1925 Launched on April 25th for equal joint owners Clifford Edward Strowger and Alfred Willie Wilkinson, both of Gorleston.

1925 Registered on June 27th as YH141.

1930 In March, whilst hauling in the nets at around midnight about 5 miles from the Isle of Man, the net appeared very heavy and under the strain the foremast broke and crashed down on to the deck. Fortunately, the crew jumped cleared as the mast came down. The nets were full of fish which were reported at the time to be of an "inedible nature".

1935 Landed a good shot of 200 crans of prime herring at Yarmouth on October 14th.

1939 Requisitioned for naval service as a minesweeper (Pennant No. FY738) during October 1939, and allocated to Dover Command.

1940 During late May took part in Operation Dynamo (the evacuation of Dunkirk).

1945 Released by the Admiralty and returned to her owners in October.

1946 On March 6th she was re-registered LT180 having been acquired by the East Briton Fishing Co. Ltd., Lowestoft. Her Yarmouth registry had been closed on February 28th.

1952 Whilst lying in the Hamilton Dock, Lowestoft on October 24th, she was struck by lightning resulting in 2ft. of her foremast being destroyed.

1955 Reported overdue on March 28th whilst mackerel fishing from Newlyn.

1955 Registry closed on September 28th.

The loss of the *Playmates*

With Skipper William Jenner DSC in charge and his crew of ten, the *Playmates* left Newlyn on Tuesday March 22nd 1955 on a fishing trip to the mackerel grounds off Ireland. Shortly after leaving port, she made a radio call and this was the last known contact that was ever made with the vessel. A sighting of her was reported on the evening of March 22nd when she was 40 - 50 miles west-north-west of Seven Stones lightship by a vessel in the same vicinity. However, with deteriorating visibility combined with worsening weather it was difficult to positively identify the vessel concerned as being the *Playmates*.

On Monday March 28th 1955, she was officially reported overdue and a search by aircraft from Pembroke Dock and Plymouth, naval vessels, fishing and other vessels which included the Lowestoft based Ministry of Agriculture and Fisheries research vessel *Platessa* commenced. Gales reaching up to 96 mph were reported in the area of the Fastnet fishing grounds off the south west coast of Ireland, where the *Playmates* was believed to have been heading. After an extensive search of the area where the vessel was likely to have been, the only trace found of the *Playmates* was part of her small boat. Following the discovery of this, it was concluded that the *Playmates* and her crew must have been overwhelmed on or about the night of Tuesday March 22nd 1955 by the state of the sea together with the force of the wind.

A memorial service for the crew of the *Playmates* was held at the Lowestoft Sailors' and Fishermen's Bethel in Lowestoft on Sunday April 17th 1955. The cover of the Order of Service, which includes the names of those that perished with the loss of the vessel, is on the next page.

Playmates leaving Yarmouth with her original registration of YH141.
Malcolm White Collection

Playmates leaving Lowestoft on a fishing trip.
Malcolm White Collection

The research vessel LT205 *Platessa* which was involved in the search for the *Playmates*.
Richards Shipbuilders - Cyril Richards Archive (1998)

MEMORIAL SERVICE

TO THE

SKIPPER AND CREW

OF THE

"PLAYMATES"

PRESUMED LOST AT SEA 22nd MARCH, 1955

HELD IN

LOWESTOFT SAILORS' AND FISHERMEN'S BETHEL

BATTERY GREEN ROAD,

Sunday 17th April, 1955

at 6-30 p.m.

WILLIAM JENNER, D.S.C., *Skipper*.

JACK HUBBARD, *Mate*.	SAMUEL COLLYER, *Chief Engineer*.
STANLEY L. BARNARD, *Hawsman*.	HARRY GOATE, *Stoker*.
GEORGE ELLIS, *Whaleman*.	SAMUEL J. COLE, *Net Stower*.
DOMINIC BROGAN, *Cast-Off*.	GEORGE INGRAM, *Net Ropeman*.
GEORGE PRETTYMAN, *Cook*.	KENNETH PAGE, *Spare Hand*.

In attendance with the families of the above-named,

HIS WORSHIP THE MAYOR OF LOWESTOFT,
ALDERMAN J. M. LANG, J.P.,
AND MEMBERS OF THE BOROUGH COUNCIL.

The front cover of the Order of Service used at the Bethel on Sunday April 17th 1955.
(Reduced in size for inclusion in this book)
Malcolm White Collection.

****
Motor trawler LT404 *British Columbia*
Sank at sea following a collision in 1957 with no casualties.

British Columbia at sea off Lowestoft on trials after a refit.
Courtesy Colne Shipping Co. Ltd. (2000)

Vessel Details
Built - 1935
Shipbuilder - Richards Ironworks Ltd., Crown Works, Lowestoft. (Yard No. 250)
Official No. 162901
Call Sign - GLRJ
Construction - Steel
Dimensions (feet) - 100.8 x 21.1 x 8.4
Tonnage - 50nett / 134gross
Engine Type - 6cylinder 310hp Diesel.
Engine Builder - Ruston & Hornsby, Lincoln.

Brief History

1935 Built for Grimsby Motor Trawlers Ltd., Henderson St., Grimsby and entered service as the side trawler GY153 *British Columbia*.
1935 Considered to be the first successful large British diesel trawler.
1939 Acquired by the Admiralty for anti-submarine duties and renamed HMS *Guava*. Allocated the pennant number T118.
1946 Purchased by Mr. G. H. Claridge, White Cottage, Water End, Wheathampstead and re-registered as GY272 *Guava*.
1949 Ownership transferred to the Colne Fishing Co., Ltd., Lowestoft and re-registered as LT404 *British Columbia*.
1952 Ownership transferred to the Clan Steam Fishing Co. (Grimsby) Ltd., Lowestoft.
1957 Vessel sank in the North Sea following a collision with an American warship.

The loss of the *British Columbia*

The *British Columbia* left Lowestoft on Friday September 27th 1957 with Skipper Martin Foley in charge, on a scheduled fishing trip which would include trawling in an area south east of the Dogger Bank. At 4.13am on Sunday September 29th the trawler was hit by the United States destroyer *Purdy* which was in formation with eleven other destroyers and the large aircraft carriers *Forrestal* and *Saratoga*. All had been involved in a NATO exercise. The *British Columbia*, which was about 120 miles from Flamborough Head, finally sank at 5.27am after all the crew had taken to a liferaft. They were picked up by one of the United States vessels and returned to the UK. The stem of the *Purdy* was pierced on the waterline and she proceeded to Portland for repairs. Information about the incident was supplied by the United States Information Service but communications between them, the owners and relatives of the crew members left much to be desired. First news of the *British Columbia's* loss came to the ten families with relatives on board through the BBC news at 1.00pm. At this time the owners knew nothing about it. Later Skipper Foley, who lived at 3 Normandy Road, Lowestoft, did make contact with Mr. Aubrey Moore by radio telephone. Mr. Moore was assistant manager of East Coast Fish Sales, a company associated with the vessel's owners, and a well known Football League referee. Skipper Foley told Mr. Moore: "We were holed on the port side and the trawler sank, but all the crew are safe." At once Mr. Moore set about contacting the relatives of the crew, but most had already been reassured by the messages broadcast by the BBC about the crew of the *British Columbia*. Recalling the moment when the trawler was struck, Skipper Foley said "Most of the crew were knocked out of their bunks and those that were not, floated out". He went on to say: "The crew took to the liferafts and, despite 6ft to 10ft. waves and a 25mph wind, they were picked up almost immediately."

Three crew members of the *British Columbia* received superficial injuries in the collision. These were third hand Mr. R. Nixon, 56 Beresford Road with minor contusions of the back, deckie learner Mr. D. Schapello, London, but staying at 13 Clapham Road with abrasions of the right index finger, and Chief Engineer Mr. R. Spurgeon, 60 Homefield Avenue, with abrasions on the left leg. Other members of the crew were the mate, Mr. Ted Sharman, 53 Stanford Street, Lowestoft; deckhands Mr. B. Utting, 10 Oakland Terrace, Kessingland; Mr. K. Wright, 11 Oakwood Road, Lowestoft and Mr. A. Turner, 23 Sycamore Avenue, Oulton Broad; cook Mr. W. Kydd, 14 St. Leonard's Road, Lowestoft; and second engineer Mr. E. Botwright, 45 Myloden Road, Lowestoft.

The British Columbia at Richards Ironworks in 1935.
Richards Shipbuilders - Cyril Richards Archive (1998)

****

Motor Fishing Vessel LO488 *Susan M.*

Lost at sea with her entire crew in 1957.

The Susan M. outward bound from Lowestoft and rigged as a trawler.
Richards Shipbuilders - Cyril Richards Archive (1998)

Vessel Details

Built - 1945
Shipbuilder - Berthon Boat Co Ltd., Lymington.
Official No. - 181892
Call Sign - MAWF
Construction - Wood
Dimensions (feet) - 75.5 x 19.75 x 9.5
Tonnage - 32nett / 73gross
Engine Type - 4 cylinder 160 hp Diesel
Engine Builder - Lister Blackstone Ltd., Dursley, Gloucestershire

Brief History

1945 Ordered in December 1944 and completed in November 1945 as MFV1223 to a standard wartime Admiralty motor fishing vessel (MFV) design.
1946 Purchased by Metcalf Motor Coasters Ltd., 4 New London Street, London EC3.
1947 Converted for use as a fishing vessel and registered as LO488 *Susan M.*
1947 Managed at Lowestoft by Hobsons Ltd., a subsidiary of trawler and drifter owners Small & Co. (Lowestoft) Ltd.
1947 - 57 Working from Lowestoft as a trawler and for several years during the autumn herring season, as a drifter.
1957 Lost with all hands east of Great Yarmouth in December 1957, presumed destroyed by a wartime mine.

The loss of the *Susan M.*

Under Skipper C. H. Conolly, the *Susan M.* left Lowestoft on Monday November 25th 1957 just after midday. Previously he had told Skipper Jenner of the drifter/trawler *Comrades* that he intended to head east for around 1½ hours, before commencing fishing. It was presumed that Skipper Conolly would trawl for three hours in a northerly direction with the ebb tide in his favour. He then intended to head further east for the Brown Ridges fishing grounds. No further contact was made with the *Susan M.* after she left Lowestoft. At around 1730hrs a loud explosion was heard by many people in Great Yarmouth including the Coastguard, and an explosion and a brilliant red flash was reported by the Cross Sand lightship on station almost 8 miles east of Great Yarmouth. The Cross Sand also reported that the flash appeared to be about 6 miles south of her position. The Gorleston lifeboat, under Coxswain Paul Williment, put to sea to investigate the unexplained explosion, and the flash reported by the Cross Sand lightship and after a "really good look round" returned to port after a search lasting four hours. The lifeboat searched up to six miles south-south-east of the Cross Sand lightship and went up to three miles further south without finding or seeing anything. The next day a Shackleton aircraft of RAF Coastal Command undertook a comprehensive search of the area but found nothing, and shipping in the area had been asked to look out for the *Susan M.*, or possibly any wreckage that could have come from her.

On December 6th 1957, Mr. R. G. Cartwright, representing the managers of the *Susan M.* was interviewed by a press reporter and stated "Although this is of course, conjecture, all the known facts suggest that *Susan M.* trawled a mine and was blown to pieces. My view is that what happened was that Skipper Conolly, in charge of the *Susan M.*, got his trawl down and probably trawled a mine of some sort. When he hauled the trawl the mine probably caught one of its horns either in the trawl warp or it hit the hull of the vessel and exploded. It would mean the instantaneous destruction of the *Susan M.* and tragically the loss of the crew". He continued "One must stress of course this is all conjecture, and we can say nothing for certain, till say, some wreckage or some other object is found. The air search going on today may possibly help".

Another official connected with the fishing industry added "The danger from mines exists and may exist for many years. There are areas off the coast of Denmark and Holland which are known as "Declared Danger Areas" and which are closed to trawling. There is a type of ground mine which is almost unsweepable. Then there was a mine barrier off our own coast and it must be conceded that it was impossible to sweep away every one". Earlier on December 6th, Mr. Cartwright and a representative of Metcalf Motor Coasters had visited all the relatives of the seven men in the vessel's crew and explained the mine theory.

The seven crew members of the *Susan M.* were Skipper C. H. Conolly, Mate J. Fisher, Third Hand G. Gilby, First Engineer B. Emmerson, Second Engineer J. McKechnie, Cook G. Howlett and Deckhand J. Conolly. All came from Lowestoft apart from the First and the Second Engineers who both lived in Carlton Colville, and the Cook who came from Beccles.

On December 10th 1957, the following announcement appeared in Lloyds List:-

SUSAN M. - London Dec. 9th - Lowestoft trawler *Susan M.*, which left Lowestoft on November 25th and has not been heard of since, is now presumed lost with all hands. It is thought that the vessel may have trawled a mine and was blown up.

A memorial service for those lost with the *Susan M.* was held in the town on December 15th 1957 details of which can be found in the next column.

Susan M. as a herring drifter about to enter Lowestoft harbour on return from the fishing grounds in 1947-48.
Courtesy Small & Co. (Lowestoft) Ltd. (2001)

MEMORIAL SERVICE

TO THE

SKIPPER AND CREW

OF THE

"SUSAN M."

PRESUMED LOST AT SEA 25th NOVEMBER, 1957

HELD IN THE

LOWESTOFT SAILORS' AND FISHERMEN'S

BETHEL

BATTERY GREEN ROAD

SUNDAY, 15th DECEMBER, 1957

at 6-30 p.m.

———

C. H. CONOLLY, *Skipper*

J. FISHER, *Mate*	B. EMMERSON, *1st Engineer*
G. GILBY, *3rd Hand*	J. McKECHNIE, *2nd Engineer*
G. HOWLETT, *Cook*	J. CONOLLY, *Deck Hand*

———

In attendance with the families of the above-named
His Worship The Mayor of Lowestoft,
Councillor L. A. Rhodes, J.P.,
and Members of the Borough Council.

The front cover of the Order of Service used at the Bethel on Sunday December 15th 1957.
(Reduced in size for inclusion in this book)
Malcolm White Collection

Lowestoft Fishing Vessels Remembered - *Section Two*

****

Motor Trawler LT323 *Faithful Star*

Broken up at Orford Ness after grounding there in 1957 with no casualties.

The *Faithful Star* leaving Lowestoft on fishing trip in the mid 1950s.
Left - Approaching the pier heads. **Right** - Heading for the open sea.
Both photographs copyright Mr. John Wells (Wells Photographic)

Vessel Details (as a motor trawler)

Built - 1927
Shipbuilder - Cochrane & Sons Ltd., Selby.
Official No. - 149197
Call Sign - GZLZ
Construction - Steel
Dimensions (feet) - 90.3 x 19.05 x 9.25
Tonnage - 49.88nett / 109.14gross
Engine Type - 3 cylinder 360hp Diesel
Engine Builder - W. H. Podd Ltd., Lowestoft (Engine fitted by A.K. Diesels Ltd.)

Brief History

1927 Built for the Star Drift Fishing Co. Ltd., Lowestoft and entered service as the steam drifter/trawler LT323 *Faithful Star*.
1934 Suffered a broken mizzen mast off Hartlepool on August 20th.
1934 Ran aground at Saltburn on September 14th.
1936 Damaged after hitting a submerged object off Dungeness on September 23rd.
1939 Towed the Lowestoft steam trawler *Tresco* into Fleetwood on March 30th.
1939 Requisitioned in September by the Admiralty for naval service as an auxiliary patrol vessel.
1946 Returned to owners in March.
1952 Underwent conversion from steam to diesel power at Lowestoft.
1955 In collision with m.v. *Dryburgh* 35 miles north east of Cromer, although suffering stem damage she continued on to the fishing grounds.
1957 Ran aground at Orford Ness and eventually broken up for scrap at that location.

The loss of the *Faithful Star*

Whilst seeking shelter in difficult sea and weather conditions off Orford Ness on Saturday December 14th 1957, at around 8.00pm the *Faithful Star*, under Skipper George Challis, was driven ashore and on to the beach. All of the crew managed to get ashore but the skipper was rescued by breeches buoy. Arrangements for a salvage attempt were made using the Great Yarmouth tug *Richard Lee Barber*, but this was delayed. The *Faithful Star* was driven further up the beach by the onshore wind and the heavy seas, leading to her becoming firmly embedded in the sand and shingle. She suffered considerable damage and was broken up on the beach after being declared a total loss. The crew of the *Faithful Star* at the time of the grounding was stated in the local press as: Skipper George Challis, Mate Jack Bessey, Chief Engineer Charles O' Neil, Second Engineer Eric Burwood, Third Hand Robert Norman, Cook Frank Webb, Deckhand Stanley Humphries and Deckhand Kenneth Womack.

Left - The *Faithful Star* on the beach at Orford Ness. She was destined to never leave that location and was cut up for scrap there. Within a few weeks there no trace of the trawler having been on the beach. *Photographer Ernest Graystone / Copyright Malcolm White* **Right** - It was hoped the tug *Richard Lee Barber* would provide assistance to the *Faithful Star* but she was delayed in arriving due to already being employed in taking a disabled barge to Harwich. *Courtesy Past Time Prints*

Lowestoft Fishing Vessels Remembered - *Section Two*

****
Motor Fishing Vessel LT369 *Frandor*
Caught fire, abandoned and sank in 1961 with no casualties.

Frandor crossing the Waveney Dock as she sets out on a fishing trip in early 1961.
Malcolm White Collection

Vessel Details
Built - 1945
Shipbuilder - Richard Irvin & Sons, Peterhead,
Official No. - 302387
Call Sign - N/A
Construction - Wood
Dimensions (feet) - 75.5 x 19.4 x 8.9
Tonnage - 28.74nett / 68.79gross
Engine Type - 4 cylinder 160 hp Diesel
Engine Builder - Lister Blackstone Ltd., Dursley, Gloucestershire.

Brief History

1945 Ordered in February 1944 and completed in January 1945 as MFV1106 to a standard wartime Admiralty motor fishing vessel (MFV) design.
1960 Purchased by G. F. Hare of Wisbech with the intention of converting the vessel to a trawler.
1960 Following conversion at Lowestoft, MFV 1106 was registered as LT369 *Frandor*
1961 Whilst fishing in the North Sea an explosion occurred and the vessel caught fire. She was abandoned by her crew and later sank.

The loss of the *Frandor*

At 2.59pm GMT on Friday April 21st 1961, the Post Office Radio Station at North Foreland received a Mayday distress call from the Lowestoft trawler *Frandor*. The message stated that the *Frandor* was on fire following an explosion in the engine room and the crew were preparing to launch the small boat. The position of the trawler was given as four miles south-west of Smiths Knoll. A further call was received at 3.10pm stating that the *Frandor* was blazing and the crew were also lowering the liferafts into the sea. A request was made for assistance from the Lowestoft or Gorleston lifeboat. The next message was received at 3.16pm when the Chief Engineer of the *Frandor* said he thought that the fuel tanks would blow up at anytime and said he was taking to the small boat or a liferaft. By 3.21pm the position of the *Frandor* had worsened when it was reported that the vessel was well alight below decks and the crew were in the small boat. The message also stated that the trawler had not been totally abandoned and the crew were alongside and would "stay to see how things were going". The next call to North Foreland was received at 3.24pm, this came from the Great Yarmouth trawler *Ocean Dawn* which stated it was going to pick up the crew and that the Dutch tug *Titan* was in attendance. The Lowestoft trawler *Filby Queen* called North Foreland at 3.31pm to say that the Skipper of the *Frandor* had abandoned her in view of the worsening conditions on the trawler. The *Ocean Dawn* was by now four to fives miles south west of Smiths Knoll and two to three miles from the blazing *Frandor*. By 3.52pm *Ocean Dawn* was not far from the *Frandor,* and sent the message "can see two lifeboats or liferafts just clear of ship am closing to pick up survivors". At 4.00pm, the motor ship *Chantala* and the steamer *Capital* both called North Foreland Radio to give reports on the current condition of the *Frandor*. The *Capital* gave the position of the *Ocean Dawn* by Decca as 5½ miles south west by west of Smiths Knoll. To provide assistance in the rescue, the Gorleston lifeboat was launched at 4.10pm and proceeded to where the *Frandor* was on fire.

The *Ocean Dawn* reported at 4.04pm "just picked up all six men. Asked what to do about ship, she is well ablaze, standing by". *Ocean Dawn* again called North Foreland Radio at 4.32pm with up-to-date information from the rescue scene and stated "Lowestoft trawler *Annrobin* has put a line on board *Frandor* which is well ablaze, otherwise nothing else can be done. Six crew transferring to Gorleston lifeboat. Cancel Mayday; OK."
The next day, the still burning hulk of the *Frandor* foundered whilst under tow.

There were six persons on board the *Frandor* when she caught fire: Skipper George "Pinny" Colby of 23 Florence Road, Pakefield; Mr. S. Woolner, 94 Pakefield Street, Lowestoft; Mr. A. Cunningham, 9 Stanley St., Lowestoft; Mr. G. Pickess, 9 Osbourne St., Lowestoft; Mr. W. King, 188 Raglan Street, Lowestoft and Mr. R. Spurgeon, 20 Crown Street, Lowestoft.

The name *Frandor* was derived from owner's first name, Frank, and his wife's name Dora.

Note
The Post Office/BT North Foreland Radio Station mentioned above closed in 1991 and the site is now a supermarket.

Lowestoft Fishing Vessels Remembered - *Section Two*

The *Frandor* is seen in the Hamilton Dock undergoing conversion to a trawler and still displaying her MFV number in 1960.
Courtesy Small & Co. (Lowestoft) Ltd. (2001)

The burning *Frandor* several hours before she sank.
Courtesy Small & Co. (Lowestoft) Ltd. (2001)

The Yarmouth drifter/trawler YH77 *Ocean Dawn* picked up the crew of the *Frandor*.
Richards Shipbuilders - Cyril Richards Archive (1998)

The Lowestoft trawler LT203 *Annrobin* provided assistance during the incident.
Courtesy Small & Co. (Lowestoft) Ltd. (2001)

****
Motor Fishing Vessel LT225 *Kirkley*
Grounded on a sandbank and abandoned off Great Yarmouth in 1963 with no casualties.

The *Kirkley* leaving Lowestoft on a fishing trip with the wheelhouse fitted new in 1960.
Richards Shipbuilders - Cyril Richards Archive (1998)

Vessel Details
Built - 1946
Shipbuilder - Wivenhoe Shipyard, Wivenhoe
Official No. - 166702
Call Sign - MCMN
Construction - Wood
Dimensions (feet) - 93.2 x 22.4 x 9.8 (1952)
Tonnage - 49.76nett / 110.70gross
Tonnage - 49.00nett / 115.00gross (1960)
Engine Type - 4 cylinder 240hp Diesel
Engine Builder - Crossley Bros. Ltd., Openshaw, Manchester.

Brief History

1946 Ordered in September 1944 and intended to be MFV1563, a standard wartime Admiralty motor fishing vessel (MFV), but the order was cancelled and the shipbuilder sought prospective purchasers for the uncompleted vessel.
1946 Sold to Mostyn & Willey Ltd., Hull. and registered as LT225 *Kirkley* on September 28th.
1960 Owners office address changed to Mostyn & Willey Ltd., 83 High St., Cowes. IOW.
1960 Owners office address changed to Mostyn & Willey Ltd., London S.W.1. (second change in 1960).
1960 Extensively rebuilt and re-engined with 360hp 6cyl. Crossley by Richards Ironworks Ltd., Lowestoft.
1960 Underwent trials on September 1st after re-building.
1963 Grounded on a sandbank off Gt. Yarmouth and became a total loss.
1963 Registry closed on September 9th.

The loss of the *Kirkley*

At about 7.00am on Monday April 8th 1963, red flares fired from the trawler *Kirkley* were seen from the shore at Caister-on-Sea, after the vessel ran aground on the north end of Scroby Sands off Great Yarmouth. The Caister lifeboat was launched with Coxswain Jack Plummer at the helm and headed in the direction of the grounded vessel, but a coaster in the vicinity directed her to a rubber dinghy containing the trawler's crew which was in broken water south of the *Kirkley*. The lifeboat went alongside the dinghy and took the eight men off, and then proceeded with the dinghy in tow to Yarmouth harbour, where the crew were landed at the Fish Wharf. Later in the day only the wheelhouse and one of *Kirkley*'s masts were reported to be showing. The skipper of the *Kirkley* was Mr. Charles Page, of 102 Hawthorn Avenue, Lowestoft who stated "I was not on watch but in my bunk, I jumped up and stopped the engine, which was going full ahead. There was no bottom showing on the echo-sounder". He continued "We got two pumps going and tried to get her to go astern. We dropped the anchor because there was a flood tide, and we got a chain of buckets, but it was all to no good. When we tried to launch the small boat, the ship heeled over and punched a hole in the small boat's side. We then launched one of the rubber rafts and got away on that". Skipper Page continued: "The lee deck was awash and water was up to the top bunks in the cabin. The only thing that kept us afloat was the fact that we were grounded". In addition to Skipper Page, other Lowestoft men on the trawler at the time of the incident were: Mr. David Whitham of 110 St. Peter's Street: David Jones, 13 Payne Street: James Barnard, 17 Southfield Gardens and Alf Butcher, of 77 Norwich Road. Crew members not from Lowestoft were Raymond Waters of Roseville, Green Lane, Kessingland: Fred Ledner, 67 Priory Road, Milford Haven: and William Potter, of 7 Laurel Avenue, Fleetwood. Upon arrival at Yarmouth the eight crew members were given baths and meals at the Yarmouth Shipwrecked Sailors Home. An investigation lasting three days into the loss of the *Kirkley* was held at Lowestoft Town Hall in November 1963. The team investigating the cause of how the vessel came to finish up wrecked on the Scroby Sands comprised the Wreck Commissioner, Mr. H. V. Brandon, and three assessors, Capt. J. Wells, Capt. F. F. Jackson and Mr. W. J. Wood. The ruling of the inquiry was that the loss of the trawler was due to "the wrongful act or default" of the skipper and second hand who were "seriously to blame" for errors of navigation.

The *Kirkley* on Scroby Sands where she soon started to break up after being battered by heavy seas. She had been rebuilt in 1960.
Richards Shipbuilders - Cyril Richards Archive (1998)

****

Motor Trawler LT182 *Tobago*

Ran aground near Lowestoft harbour mouth in 1964 with no casualties. Later refloated and scrapped.

The Tobago makes for the harbour mouth as she leaves on a fishing trip.
Malcolm White Collection

Vessel Details

Built - 1950
Shipbuilder - Cochrane & Sons Ltd. Selby (Yard No. 993)
Official No. 183935
Call Sign - MGZF
Construction - Steel
Dimensions (feet) - 107.8 x 21.15 x 10.35
Tonnage - 62.9nett / 168.48gross
Engine Type - 6cylinder 420hp Diesel.
Engine Builder - Ruston & Hornsby, Lincoln.

Brief History

1950 Built for the Milford Steam Trawling Co. Ltd. and entered service as the side trawler M128 *Milford Countess*.
1955 Sold to the Colne Fishing Co. Ltd., Lowestoft.
1955 Identity changed briefly to LT182 *Milford Countess* before receiving her new name of *Tobago*.
1955 Registered at Lowestoft on April 26th 1955.
1964 Grounded north of Lowestoft harbour entrance, later refloated and sold for scrap.

The loss of the *Tobago*

Whilst returning from a fishing trip in bad weather on Thursday March 19th 1964, the *Tobago* went ashore at around 4.00am very close to the harbour entrance at Lowestoft. The vessel was stranded in a small area of shingle/sandy beach on the North Pier Extension and for several weeks proved to be a major attraction for sightseers and maritime enthusiasts since the trawler was easily accessible. She was refloated on Wednesday April 29th and taken into Lowestoft harbour where reusable equipment and parts were removed prior to her leaving the port for a shipbreaker's yard. *Tobago* was towed away from Lowestoft by the trawler *Togo* which was also going to be scrapped at the same yard.

Left - The day after she ran ashore, *Tobago* on the beach not far from the harbour entrance at Lowestoft.
Right - On her way to the shipbreakers after being refloated and stripped of anything of use including the engine. Taking the part of a tug is the much smaller trawler *Togo*, also making her final voyage. The date is Thursday October 8th 1964.
Copyright John Wells (Wells Photographic)

Lowestoft Fishing Vessels Remembered - *Section Two*

****

Motor Trawler LT432 *Boston Pionair*
Lost at sea with her entire crew in 1965.

A view from the South Pier at Lowestoft showing the *Boston Pionair*
turning in the Outer Harbour.
Richards Shipbuilders - Cyril Richards Archive (1998)

Vessel Details (as a trawler)
Built - 1956
Shipbuilder - Richards Ironworks Ltd., Crown Works, Lowestoft. (Yard No. 429)
Official No. 187846
Call Sign - GSMM
Construction - Steel
Dimensions (feet) - 103.0 x 22.42 x 10.9
Tonnage - 55.47nett / 165.85gross
Engine Type - 5cylinder 550hp Diesel
Engine Builder - H. Widdop & Co. Ltd., Keighley (Associated British Engineering)

Brief History

1956 Launched on May 13th for the Pegasus Trawling Co. Ltd., Fleetwood as the side trawler FD96 *Boston Pionair*
1956 Ran trials on July 9th.
1962 Re-registered on July 6th as LT432.
1965 Total loss with all her crew after foundering in the North Sea.

The Loss of the *Boston Pionair*

On February 6th 1965 the *Boston Pionair* under Skipper Brian Moyse and with a crew of eight left Lowestoft with other trawlers, including *Boston Widgeon* and *Roy Stevens* and headed for the Horn Reef area and the tail of the Dogger Bank, where they fished for the next six days. On Friday February 12th at 6.00pm, the B.B.C. broadcast a warning of Force 10 winds; the weather got worse during that evening and according to Skipper William Deacon of *Boston Widgeon* at the Court of Inquiry into the loss of the *Boston Pionair*, became a "good force ten".

With the fishing trip nearly at a close and as they were a long way from home it was agreed by the three skippers that they should move further westwards. While the *Boston Widgeon* and *Roy Stevens* had another haul, the *Boston Pionair* was seen by Skipper Deacon to get her gear on board and at about 7.20pm set off in a south-southwest direction. Skipper Deacon then lost visual contact of the *Boston Pionair* and she was never positively seen again.

An unconfirmed report from the Lowestoft trawler *Wroxham Queen* stated that a vessel, which could have been the missing trawler, was seen at 10.00pm on Sunday February 14th at latitude 55°15'N., longitude 2°20'E.

On Saturday February 13th, the weather was very bad and *Boston Widgeon* continued on her course with Skipper Deacon hearing on two occasions radio messages from the *Boston Pionair*. The *Boston Pionair* was on a more westerly course than *Boston Widgeon* and Skipper Deacon heard Skipper Moyse say that he expected to sight the drilling rig *Mister Cap* that was in the area. By tea time, Skipper Deacon decided to slow the *Boston Widgeon* down to "dodging speed"; it was not his policy to "lay-on" to the seas. Bad weather continued on Sunday 14th when there were very high seas and winds of force nine or ten. The skippers of the *Boston Widgeon* and *Boston Pionair* were talking to each other at about 6.30am on the radio, and Skipper Moyse asked Skipper Deacon how he was getting on, Skipper Deacon replied that he was still dodging. When asked how he was getting on, Skipper Moyse said he had been "laying-to" for 1½ hours and that "by the look of the weather he would have to start dodging again soon". After that he said "over" and Skipper Deacon answered with more conversation about the fishing and then said "over", he expected to get an answer, but none came. However, the skipper of the *Roy Stevens* who heard the conversation stated that he thought Skipper Moyse signed off in the normal way. After waiting a while Skipper Deacon tried to call the *Boston Pionair* but received no reply. He then contacted the skipper of the *Roy Stevens* and asked if he could try and make contact with the *Boston Pionair* since he believed she was nearer to the *Boston Pionair* than the *Boston Widgeon*. The *Roy Stevens* tried unsuccessfully to make contact with the *Boston Pionair* as did the *Boston Widgeon* again later in the day and in the evening. The next day, Monday February 15th, Skipper Deacon reported to the owners that he and the *Roy Stevens* could not contact the *Boston Pionair*. The next day, the owners asked Humber Radio to alert all shipping about the *Boston Pionair* and at approximately 2.00pm, a small boat and a lifebuoy were picked up by the French trawler *La Fayette*, both having come from the *Boston Pionair*. In addition to the items picked up by the French trawler, wreckage positively identified as coming from the *Boston Pionair*, was picked up by trawlers and other vessels involved in the search. A significant find late on the 16th was an empty 12 man liferaft which was picked up by Canadian destroyer HMCS *Columbia*; the serial number on the liferaft was that of one of those carried by the missing trawler.

On Wednesday February 17th, the owners of the missing trawler issued a statement that included a list of the items that had been picked up, this included the small boat, an inflatable liferaft, lifebuoys and several items of wreckage positively identified as coming from the *Boston Pionair*. Another press release on February 17th, stated that it was believed the missing trawler was making for the Dogger Bight, about 70 miles north-east of Scarborough at the time she sent her last message. Several aircraft and naval vessels were involved in the search including the anti-submarine frigates HMS *Murray* and HMS *Brighton* and the coastal minesweeper HMS *Brereton;* she took over the search in the Dogger Bank area from the inshore minesweeper HMS *Dingley* early on Thursday February 18th. Also on the 18th, Cromer Coastguards requested that all shipping look-out for the other orange coloured 12 man liferaft from the trawler that had so far not been found.

A further development on Thursday February 18th was the important announcement by Gorleston Coastguards that the search for the *Boston Pionair* and her crew would be discontinued at 5.00pm and this information was broadcast to all shipping at 5.30pm. It was announced by Lloyds of London on Wednesday March 10th 1965 that the *Boston Pionair* was officially listed as a "missing vessel", and stated that the trawler last reported by radio at 6.30am on Sunday February 14th when about 16 miles north-west of the drilling rig *Mister Cap*, which was located in latitude 55° 3'N., longitude 2° 40'E.

The Memorial Service for the crew was conducted by the Port Missionary, Mr. James Kirby, and was held at the Bethel on Sunday February 28th 1965. It was attended by over 600 people including relatives and friends of the crew, the Mayor and Mayoress, Mr. and Mrs. D. G. Hayden, members of the Borough Council, Mr. Jim Prior, M.P. for Lowestoft, representatives of the fishing industry and of two nautical societies. In order to accommodate all those attending, a closed circuit television link was set up to a room at the side of the Bethel.

The next day the trawler *Boston Pegasus*, a sister ship to the *Boston Pionair*, took over 150 wreaths to the north of the Dogger Bank to be placed on the sea near the last known position of the lost trawler. Before the trawler sailed the wreaths were blessed by the Rev. D. C. Bartle, Vicar of St. John's Church and the Last Post was sounded by two trumpeters of the Royal Anglian Regiment.

In addition to the memorial service held in Lowestoft, a service was also held at Mundesley and two deckhands on another trawler arranged their own personal tribute.

The service at Mundesley saw the largest congregation seen for many years at All Saints' Church assembled for the memorial service held for 27 year old Michael Lee. Amongst the congregation of around 500 were a large number of immediate mourners, the coxswains of both Cromer lifeboats, local fishermen from Mundesley and Cromer, Coastguards, and several parish councillors. The Rev. J. Gedge conducted the service and the collection was sent to the appeal opened by the Mayor of Lowestoft, Mr. Hayden.

An anchor of flowers was cast upon the sea from the Lowestoft trawler *Grenada* by two deckhands who knew two of those lost on the *Boston Pionair*, Michael Lark and Billy Stebbing. The deckhands, Paul Carver and Daniel Sturley, said they wanted to pay their own tribute to two of their friends who they had been at school with. The *Grenada* left Grimsby on a fishing trip complete with the anchor of flowers on board.

MEMORIAL SERVICE

TO THE

SKIPPER AND CREW

OF THE

"BOSTON PIONAIR"

PRESUMED LOST AT SEA 14th FEBRUARY, 1965

HELD IN THE

LOWESTOFT SAILORS' AND FISHERMEN'S BETHEL

BATTERY GREEN ROAD

SUNDAY, 28th FEBRUARY, 1965

at 6.30 p.m.

BRIAN MOYSE, Skipper

GORDON BEAMISH, Mate	ANTHONY THURSTON, 1st Engineer
MICHAEL LARK, 3rd Hand	WALTER THURSTON, 2nd Engineer
BERT MOYSE, Cook	JOHN GENERY, Deck Hand
MICHAEL LEE, Deck Hand	WILLIAM STEBBING, Deck Hand

In attendance with the families of the above-named
His Worship The Mayor of Lowestoft,
Councillor D. G. HAYDEN, J.P.,
Members of the Borough Council
and Mr. JIM PRIOR, M.P.

The front cover of the Order of Service used at the Bethel on Sunday February 28th 1965.
(Reduced in size for inclusion in this book)
Malcolm White Collection

The Boston Pegasus leaves Lowestoft and heads for the Dogger Bank area with over 150 wreaths.
Richards Shipbuilders - Cyril Richards Archive (1998)

The three day Court of Inquiry into the loss of the *Boston Pionair* commenced on Tuesday November 30th 1965 at Lowestoft and was conducted by the Wreck Commissioner, Mr. J. V. Naisby assisted by two assessors, Mr. A. Lyndsay and Mr. D. A. Roberts. The Board of Trade was represented by Mr. Barry Sheen and Mr. A. P. Clarke and the trawler's owners, the Pegasus Trawling Co. Ltd., by Mr. W. Porges Q.C. and Mr. B. F. Stone. A model of the *Boston Herald*, a sister ship to the *Boston Pionair* was shown at the inquiry together with three lifebuoys, a boat hook, three of the fish room hatches and a piece of the wheelhouse grating all confirmed as coming from the missing trawler.

For the Board of Trade, Mr. Sheen stated that their case into the loss of the trawler was that the stability of the *Boston Pionair* was certainly undesirably low, and perhaps it might be proper to describe it as inadequate to meet conditions reasonably to be expected in the North Sea in February. "In saying that, I am not suggesting that there was any fault of the owners. I am not suggesting any criticism of the owners because in the last ten years there have been substantial advances in knowledge of this subject" he said.

At the inquiry several skippers gave evidence including Skipper Deacon who was asked about the practice of "laying-on" which some skippers did in bad weather. Skipper Deacon commented that he would not have laid a ship broadside where he was on the night the *Boston Pionair* was lost, because he considered it to be too dangerous. Skipper Deacon was also asked about the radio silence from the *Boston Pionair* and said he thought it possible that her aerial had come down or was damaged, but when she failed to respond to the 6.00pm rendezvous call he was rather concerned since a damaged aerial should have been repaired by then. He said that there were waves 35 - 40 feet high and there was "a really bad roll".

Skipper Deacon, who skippered the *Boston Pionair* before Skipper Moyse took over in October 1963, said: "I found she was a very good ship and I had no complaints about her at all."

Skipper Victor Crisp, junior, of Lound was skipper of the *Boston Victor* when the *Boston Pionair* was lost, and said he was dodging from about 8.00pm on the Friday until about 5.00pm on Sunday. He was ten miles west of the drilling rig *Mister Cap* and every two hours was in radio contact with the Lowestoft trawler *Wroxham Queen*. "It was that type of weather when you feel happier having a chum about" he said. The worst weather was during the Saturday night when there were gusts of up to force eleven.

When told of the search for the *Boston Pionair*, Skipper Crisp set off for the area where he knew Skipper Moyse often fished. He was then informed that an upturned lifeboat had been seen and was guided to the location by a searching RAF Shackleton reconnaissance aircraft which had sighted the lifeboat earlier. However the French trawler *La Fayette* was already in the area and had the *Boston Pionair's* small boat on her deck. The small boat had been picked up by the French trawler at about 2.00pm on February 16th. Skipper Crisp went on board the French trawler and was shown on a chart where the boat and some wreckage was found. The French skipper would not let Skipper Crisp have the *Boston Pionair's* small boat, but gave him a lifebuoy from the missing trawler. With daylight fading, Skipper Crisp went to the area indicated by the French skipper where he had found the lifeboat and searched for any further wreckage without success.

A representative of the National Institute of Oceanography, Mr. L. Draper, stated that during the storm the probable height of the highest waves at intervals of around ten minutes was about 35ft. and the highest wave of all would probably be about 46ft. Over the Dogger Bank there would be more "breaking waves" than in deeper water and it was estimated these would be travelling at 23knots at 60ft depth. Actual conditions could be about 20% above or below this estimate.

The Wreck Commissioner, Mr. Naisby Q.C., described the extensive air and sea search in which 50 trawlers, other ships and several aircraft were involved and reported that one of the aircraft saw wreckage and bodies but when rescue ships arrived at that location they found nothing. He went on to praise Skipper Crisp for his efforts in the search and said that the chances of being able to do anything other than pick up wreckage were nil from what the Court had been told. If a search had been started earlier the result would have probably met with the same result, but the merit of what one does is not always in results.

The *Lowestoft Lady* under Skipper Michael Reynolds of Woods Loke, Lowestoft, was also at sea when her sister ship, the *Boston Pionair*, was lost. He described how the *Lowestoft Lady* was not taking any water and how the mate went down on deck to see to some netroom wedges which had come loose. "I was keeping an eye on the mate, and as he started to come up towards the wheelhouse again I saw him running" he said. "When I looked out of the wheelhouse, I saw what was coming - a freak wave. This was a wave bigger than the normal swell, we tried to keep the stern into the wind. The wave broke on the corner and pushed us round and we lay broadside. As she lay broadside the next wave came on board as well. We put on full speed, put the wheel hard over and she came round and cleared herself of water."
He said that the ship had heeled over while broadside and the pressure of water broke one of the wheelhouse windows. Asked if he would attempt to run before the wind again, Skipper Reynolds replied "Normally I would not."

Mr. Barry Sheen, counsel for the Board of Trade, read affidavits showing that the radio, navigation and liferaft equipment had all been inspected and was in good order when the missing trawler left Lowestoft, and Mr. W. A. Thorpe, a ship's husband with Boston Deep Sea Fisheries, said the "*Boston Pionair* was 100 per cent perfect" when she left Lowestoft on her last trip.

Evidence of finding wreckage was given in affidavits from other skippers who were at sea on the night of the storm. David Hunt, skipper of the *Boston Beaver*, had been fishing near the Clay Deep and said he had found a wheelhouse grating, a wooden hatch cover, a broken oar, pound boards, two bobbins and pieces of grating. Michael Gamble, skipper of the *Universal Star*, described how he had seen about a dozen fishroom boards and a deckboard in the sea although there was no means of positively identifying them,

Top - The newly completed *Boston Pionair* in the Trawl Dock
Richards Shipbuilders - Cyril Richards Archive (1998)

Bottom - A North Pier view of the *Boston Pionair* approaching the harbour mouth as she leaves on a fishing trip.
Richards Shipbuilders - Cyril Richards Archive (1998)

however a lifebuoy he picked up was from the *Boston Pionair*. When asked by Mr. Porges Q. C. about the *Boston Pionair*, Mr. Alfred Boydon, marine superintendant of Boston Deep Sea Fisheries, said he had been concerned about the vessel since her keel was laid, and in 1964, a special survey was undertaken by Lloyd's. No alterations had been made that would affect her stability and her engines were more powerful than the earlier ships of her class to extend her area of fishing. He said that all seven trawlers in the class had been built to Lloyd's specification; there was no obligation to do so but it was the Boston company's policy. Mr. Porges also asked: "Apart from the *Boston Pionair* have you ever had cause to worry about any of them" – "No, not at all", was the reply.

The experiences of the *Lowestoft Lady* during the same storm were recalled at the inquiry. The one time BBC television star is seen here leaving Lowestoft on a fishing trip.
Copyright Malcolm White

Mr. Peter Catchpole, Lowestoft manager of Boston Deep Sea Fisheries, was asked about the skipper of the *Boston Pionair* and said that Skipper Moyse was appointed in September 1964. Previously he had skippered the *Boston Trident* and other vessels on occasional trips and had proven "very satisfactory." He said that before the tragedy skippers were required to report on Mondays, Wednesdays and Fridays but now each ship was ordered to report daily.
Mr. Porges asked Mr. Catchpole if they ever discussed what skippers should do in bad weather, Mr. Catchpole replied: "These skippers are experienced men. That is the reason they are put in the ships."

Mr. Sheen then read to the court a long comprehensive circular about the stability of fishing vessels and said a copy had been sent to all fishing vessel owner associations. The Commissioner commented: "Does anybody in the Board of Trade think the average skipper, if given this long document, is going to read it and understand it? These are theoretical calculations taken by some civil servant sitting in Whitehall without any regard to the practicalities of the case." When Mr. Sheen explained that a summary of the recommendations was in the last part of the circular, the Commissioner said: "If it is the last part that is important, then it is the part least likely to be read by the skippers." Mr. Catchpole said he had seen the circular and thought the first part was "a little bit baffling."
However, a synopsis of the recommendations had been put in the skippers' file and each skipper was required to read what was in the file, and then sign the file. Mr. Sheen then asked "Apparently, some Lowestoft skippers adopt the practice of laying-to; do you draw attention to the dangers of this sort of thing?" Mr. Catchpole said: "No I cannot guarantee that every skipper has read the file. Some of them religiously do so but I cannot check on every single one."

By the time the Court of Inquiry was held in November 1965, Skipper Victor Crisp had become the Lowestoft shore skipper for Boston Deep Sea Fisheries (managers of the *Boston Pionair*) and he told the Inquiry that he had been the original skipper of the *Boston Pegasus*, the first of a batch of seven trawlers of which the *Boston Pionair* was one. He told the inquiry: "I was very happy when I took her and when we were in a very heavy gale with winds between 70-80 mph she rode out the terrific seas comfortably." He added that everything was in order aboard the ill-fated trawler before she left Lowestoft for the last time. Mr. Porges asked Skipper Crisp concerning the *Boston Pionair* class of trawlers: "Have you since you have been ashore from time to time got reports from skippers when they came back from voyages in these? It is only natural you hear what weather they have had to contend with. Have you ever had any complaints from any skipper of his ship being a bad sea boat." Skipper Crisp replied: "No sir, never".

Mr. George Thomson, a senior ships surveyor in the marine safety branch, was asked about the stability of the lost trawler and her sister ships with mention being made of more ballast being put in the bottom of the vessels, increasing the freeboard and decreasing the top weight. Asked by Mr. Sheen: "Is there any way of reducing the top weight which would have an appreciable effect?" Mr. Thomson replied: "I cannot think of anything at the moment which would achieve a simple reduction without a complete rebuild."

With regard to increasing the ballast, Mr. Thomson thought this would make the trawlers uncomfortable in moderate conditions and to the question about increasing the freeboard, he said one foot increase in freeboard by increasing the depth of the vessel would be a possible means of attaining higher stability but he did not think anybody would consider this to be practicable. Asked about the cost of such an improvement, he said this would be substantial and added that no improvement could be achieved by limiting the amount of fish on board. Mr. Thomson said that the *Boston Wayfarer*, a recent addition to the Boston fleet, measured up to the standard he suggested. He thought an intelligent appreciation of comparison would give the owners the chance to see which type of vessel to select in the future.

Mr. Porges asked Mr. Thomson if he was prepared to say that the present fleet should be considered unfit for further use. Mr. Thomson replied: "I have not said that." Mr. Porges suggested that the other six sister ships to the *Boston Pionair* had an exceptionally good record in the last ten years. Mr. Thomson said but for the loss of the *Boston Pionair*, the court would not have heard of the experience of the *Lowestoft Lady* in the same storm. Following the loss of the *Boston Pionair*, he had been told of the experiences of three other vessels "which were alarming to say the least of it." He added, "One skipper was nearly drowned in the wheelhouse." To assess the seaworthiness of such vessels it would have been useful to have information of similar incidents that had happened in the last ten years but those in fishing were usually glad to get back in port and forget about them.

Mr. Thomson began his evidence by saying his investigations had shown that everything in the *Boston Pionair* had been managed in the proper order. He had had every co-operation from the owners and he considered the ill-fated trawler to be a well maintained vessel. After discussing statistical evidence concerning the *Boston Pionair*, Mr. Thomson produced graphs to illustrate stability in certain conditions. The Wreck Commissioner asked "Does it mean that the vessel could go over on beam ends and come up again." Mr. Thomson replied: "This could happen but it depends on everything being watertight."

Moving on to the experiences of the *Lowestoft Lady*, which in the same storm was said to have been caught by a "freak" wave and then turned broadside so her starboard side was submerged, he thought it likely that she had been in a similar situation to the *Boston Pionair*. He estimated that 20 tons of water had entered the engine room and another two tons had got into the crew's accommodation. "It surprised me that so much water should have entered in such a short time and that it had a less disastrous effect on the ship's stability" Mr. Thomson said. He went on to say that he reckoned the doorway to the engine room would have been submerged to a depth of 9 feet for about 10 seconds. Mr. Sheen asked what would have happened to the *Boston Pionair* had she had a similar list and had been flooded, in reply Mr. Thomson said there was a difference in the bunkers of the *Boston Pionair* and this would mean that she would suffer worse if she took the same amount of water, however, she would still have the capacity to right herself although perhaps to a lesser degree.

Mr. Thomson was then questioned on different aspects of the stability of fishing vessels including the effect of the weight of water within and on board a vessel and the ability to right herself. In the case of the *Boston Pionair*, he calculated that with 40 tons of water in the engine room and five tons in the crew's quarters and with an inclining angle of 40 degrees, she would not have returned to an upright position. Asked about a possible situation when there was 35 tons of water aboard, he said he hesitated to be positive in suggesting there was a definite limit. He was further questioned about a desirable standard of stability in such vessels. He stated that since World War Two there had been 25 vessels lost in circumstances that suggested these vessels capsized but it was possible to study the question of stability in only one in five of these cases.

The design of the *Boston Wayfarer* was seen as the way forward for future vessels. Built in 1965, the Lowestoft trawler is seen here entering her home port. *Courtesy Stanley Earl*

Following the accumulation of recent evidence (in 1965) the Board of Trade issued the comprehensive circular about the stability of fishing vessels with a copy being sent to all fishing vessel owner associations. Asked by the Wreck Commissioner if he thought the "average trawler skipper" could understand the first two pages of the circular, Mr. Thomson said: "I would say yes. I am constantly having it borne on me that skippers are very intelligent people." The Wreck Commissioner replied "They need to be". Mr. Thomson was then asked if the handling of a vessel in rough weather could affect a vessel's stability, to this question he replied: "If vessels of this category were known to be a positive danger at an angle of 45 degrees, then extreme effort should be made to resist such a list." The Wreck Commissioner, Mr. J. V. Naisby, asked Mr. Thomson what he thought about other ships of a similar design. Mr. Thomson replied: "I would say don't use them as a basis for future building." Mr. Naisby then asked if he thought that lives were being put in jeopardy by sending such vessels to sea as they were at the moment (in 1965). Mr. Thomson replied: "The casualty rate of fishing vessels of this category is something like ten vessels in ten years out of 1000 vessels at risk. Every vessel has that risk most of the time. The difference between these vessels you are questioning me about and vessels which may be somewhat better is fractional. There is no hard line between absolute safety and absolute lack of safety."

Mr. Porges, representing the owners of the missing trawler, asked Mr. Thomson if the Board of Trade had issued no document of guidance until September 1965. He agreed that the document did not suggest what owners should do with existing vessels. Mr. Porges asked: "Are you saying that you are in a position today to lay down a definite standard to which everybody must conform?" to which Mr. Thomson replied: "Yes, we are in a position to lay down a standard but the question of whether everyone must conform has not been legalised."

On the third day of the inquiry Mr. Thomson said he could see no practical difficulty in keeping the engine room door on the *Boston Pionair* class of trawler closed. There would be further benefit if the door was made watertight and "in practical terms" this could be done. Another possible step would be to make access to the deckhouse more protected. Mr. Thomson said that international discussions would be leading the Board of Trade to issue notices about the load line on trawlers. It was illogical that fishing vessels which worked in more arduous conditions than cargo ships "should not have these conditions legislated for in the matter of load line rules." The Commissioner said the court could hardly make recommendations for study of a matter which was now being considered internationally, "It is like teaching one's grandmother to suck eggs" he said.

Mr. Thomson said: "To ensure the best safety possible there would have been steel covers on the fish hatches instead of wooden covers with tarpaulins." The owner's marine superintendent, Mr Alfred Boydon, was then recalled to give an account of the steps that had been taken by the Boston company since the loss of the ill-fated trawler. He stated: "To see if anything could be done has been the uppermost thought in our minds since the tragedy occurred." He went on to say that his firm had arranged for the alley-way door to be made watertight, with clasps, and a notice to be put on it to say that it should be kept shut in bad weather. The fitting of a bulkhead across the afterpart of the fo'castle, with a similar notice, had also been ordered.

The marine superintendent added: "We have instructed a firm of naval architects to look into the possibility of improving the stability of our existing vessels." The firm was prepared to invite the Board of Trade to any "inclining" experiments carried out and seek their advice. Investigations would be carried out in the company's ships and certain of these would be given inclining tests to check their stability. He added that the company now has three new vessels which complied with Board of Trade stability standards. "But we are already having complaints from the skippers that they cannot correct the ships because they are being thrown about too much" said Mr. Boydon.

Mr. Boydon was then asked by Mr. Sheen if he would not agree that it was essential to tell skippers they should keep their ships heading into the sea in bad weather. Mr. Boydon replied that he would agree, but the operation of a ship was entirely in the skipper's hands once she had left port. The company had not issued any instructions to skippers about abandoning the practice of "laying" in bad weather. With the Inquiry drawing to a close Mr. Sheen asked the court to consider 14 questions which included:-

Was the trawler seaworthy in all respects other than stability?
Did the trawler have adequate stability?
Were all proper steps taken to initiate a search for the trawler and her crew?
What was the probable cause of the loss of the trawler?
Was the loss of the trawler caused or contributed to by the negligence of any person or persons?

Mr. Porges suggested that a court had never had to deal with a case in which the evidence of upkeep, general maintenance and care, the care of seamen and general seaworthiness had been so good. With regard to the history of the *Boston Pionair's* sister ships, this had been without blemish – indeed they had been given high recommendations from extremely reliable evidence. He went on to invite the court to answer "no" to the first question about stability, and said that it was inconceivable that the vessels of the *Boston Pionair* class had been "narrowly missing disaster" for ten years. The *Lowestoft Lady* had gone through some "pretty difficult" circumstances but although according to mathematical calculations she appeared to be near disaster, she had come through these incredible trials and was still sailing the seas. In that case the answer to the second question must be that her stability was adequate. The Commissioner said the court did not intend to lay down standards of stability. "I don't think we have got any warrant for doing it" he said. Mr. Porges contended that the evidence had shown that the owners had not hesitated for a moment to do everything possible to increase the safety of the existing fleet in consultation with the expert evidence available. Mr. Sheen said that although the stability of the *Boston Pionair* was less than the standard now suggested by the Board of Trade, the vessel might not have been lost had she maintained "watertight integrity" and that this was one of the lessons that had been learned from the investigation. If that was right, then what was wanted was a recommendation that steps should be taken, as were being taken by the owners of the *Boston Pionair,* to reduce the possibility of water entering fishing ships. He continued: "It would desirable if the court could draw attention to the opinion that "laying" was a bad practice because of the risk of getting water aboard."

On Friday January 28th 1966, the findings of the Court of Inquiry were presented by the Wreck Commissioner, Mr. J. V. Naisby Q.C. at Lowestoft.

Mr. Naisby said that as long as the hull and superstructure of the trawler remained watertight she had adequate stability with a righting level up to a large angle of keel.

Seven mouths after the loss of the trawler, the Board of Trade made certain recommendations about standards of righting levels. He continued: "In point of fact, *Boston Pionair* more than complied with the recommendations, but according to the calculations of the senior ship surveyor, did not quite have the minimum righting level suggested." Mr. Naisby said the notice issued by the Board of Trade concerned itself with many technical expressions which many fishing skippers might find difficult to understand. The recommendation of the court was that this notice should be issued in two parts, one for owners and shipbuilders dealing with design, and the other to skippers dealing with the operation of the ships.

It was concluded that the probable cause of the loss of the *Boston Pionair* was that the vessel was overwhelmed in severe weather conditions by a wave or succession of waves which caused the trawler to roll with such severity that her "righting level was extinguished and she thereby lost the ability to right herself." He added that possible damage to the hull or superstructure could not be excluded. The court recommended that all openings in the superstructure ought to be arranged so that in bad weather they could be made watertight and all skippers be advised that the maintenance of the watertight integrity of the superstructure was of primary importance to the safety of the vessel; the court also found that the loss of the *Boston Pionair* and all her crew was not caused or contributed to by the negligence of any person.

The *Boston Widgeon,* seen here off Lowestoft, was one of the other two trawlers that left Lowestoft with the *Boston Pionair* and were initially fishing in the same area as her.
Copyright Malcolm White

When completed in 1956 at Richards Ironworks in Lowestoft, *Boston Pionair* had the Fleetwood registration FD96. She is seen here at Lowestoft in the early 1960s with her Fleetwood registration on return from a fishing trip.
Richards Shipbuilders - Cyril Richards Archive (1998)

Notes

a) HM Coastguard stations Cromer and Gorleston - These are no longer coastguard stations, Cromer is now a private residence and Gorleston is manned by coastwatch volunteers.

b) Humber Radio - This once well known coastal radio station closed in 2000.

c) Righting Lever - A term used in the evaluation and determination of the stability and buoyancy of a ship

d) Pegasus Trawling Co. Ltd. - a subsidiary company of Boston Deep Sea Fisheries Ltd.

****
Twin Screw Motor Drifter/Trawler LT245 *J. A. P.*
Foundered at sea in 1967 with no casualties.

An early 1930s innovative twin screw design which turned out to be very successful.
Essentially as built, *J. A. P.* arrives back at Lowestoft from a fishing trip in the early 1960s.
Copyright John Wells (Wells Photographic)

Vessel Details
Built - 1931
Shipbuilder - Richards Ironworks Ltd., Crown Works, Lowestoft. (Yard No. 244)
Official No. - 162954
Call Sign - MQLV
Construction - Steel
Dimensions (feet) - 74.6 x 18.6 x 8.7
Tonnage - 40.03nett / 79.01gross.
Engine Type - 2 x 70hp diesel
Engine Builder - Deutz AG, Cologne, Germany

Brief History

1931 Built for W. H. Podd Ltd., Lowestoft and entered service as the twin screw drifter/trawler LT245 *J. A. P.* Fitted with protection gear to prevent her twin screws being fouled by drift nets.
1931 Ran trials in September and took part in the autumn herring fishing, this being the only year that she worked as a drifter.
1934 Ownership transferred to Inshore Trawlers Ltd. Lowestoft.
1936 Re-engined with two 100hp Allen diesel engines.
1937 Grounded on the Haisboro' Sands on November 14th. Floated off on the rising tide.
1940 Part of the small boat from the missing drifter/trawler LT1141 *Lord Haldane* trawled up off Caldey Island on November 15th. *J. A. P.* was fishing from Padstow at that time.
1945 One of the first two trawlers to land fish on the Lowestoft market after World War II, the other vessel being the *Pilot Jack*.
1949 Grounded on the Inner Shoal off Lowestoft on January 1st and damaged her rudder. The tug *Lowestoft* assisted in freeing the vessel and brought her into port.
1958 Sold to James Joseph Colby, Lowestoft
1960 Ownership transferred to James Joseph Colby, R. Howes and Sidney R. Bond, Lowestoft
1961 Grounded on mudflats near the slipways in the Inner Harbour at Lowestoft on January 16th.
1964 Sold to Colby Fish Selling Co. Ltd., Lowestoft.
1965 Funnel markings changed from "CHB" to "C" in April.
1965 Grounded off the South Pier at Lowestoft on October 30th. Refloated on the rising tide.
1967 Sank in the North Sea near the Smith's Knoll lightship after developing a serious leak, no casualties.

The loss of the *J. A. P.*

The *J. A.P.* left Lowestoft on the morning of Saturday February 18th 1967 intending to fish in the Smith's Knoll area.
During the following Sunday night, when the trawler was 21 miles north east of the Smith's Knoll lightship, she sprang a leak with the result that the engine room soon became flooded. With the situation on board deteriorating rapidly and having sent out the first distress call at 8.45pm, the skipper, crew and a passenger prepared to take to the liferaft. The distress calls were heard by Humber Radio which then relayed it on to shipping in the area. Several vessels answered these calls and the 8221ton Danish motor vessel *England* replied that she would go immediately to the aid of the *J. A. P.*
At 9.18pm, the *J. A. P.* reported that the *England* was alongside and that those on board were ready to push away from the side of their trawler in the liferaft and make for the Danish vessel. In the darkness, the weather conditions were worsening with almost gale force winds and a very heavy sea running. Just after 10.00pm, news came through that all the crew members and the passenger from the *J. A. P.* were safely on board the *England*, which would take them to Esbjerg, her home port.
With this good news, owner's representative Mr. James J. Colby set off to visit all the homes of relatives to tell them of the latest developments. Gorleston lifeboat, which had been launched to bring the survivors ashore, was stood down and returned to her station when she heard of the Danish vessels intentions.
The motor vessel *Actuality* reported at 10.06pm that the lights on the *J. A. P.* had gone out and she appeared to be anchored about half a mile south of the lightship. Skipper Jacklin had earlier said in a radio call that the trawler was anchored to the seabed by her trawl gear.
Those on board the *J. A. P.* at the time of her loss were given in the local press as: Skipper Clive Jacklin (37) of 107 Stradbroke Road, Pakefield, Mate David Ernest Reeder (23), 99a High Street, Lowestoft, Engineer Albert Edward Osbourne (30), 3 Compass Street, Lowestoft, Cook William Henry Page-Pipe (58), 49 Lower Olland Street, Bungay and Deckhand Robert James Rumsby (57), 3 Catherine Terrace, Pakefield. Also rescued was Mr. P. Hart (58), 10 Orford Drive, Lowestoft who had taken a trip on the trawler to see if he would like a job at sea.

The morning after the loss of the *J. A. P.*, the Trinity House vessel *Mermaid* searched in the area where the trawler was last seen but found nothing.

Lowestoft Fishing Vessels Remembered - *Section Two*

Two views of *J. A. P.* in the Outer Harbour and heading for sea. On the **left** she is seen in the 1930s when still a relatively new diesel powered trawler, and in comparison, many traditional sailing trawlers can be seen in two of the docks. *Malcolm White Collection* On the **right**, leaving for the fishing grounds in the early 1960s with her funnel markings indicating the ownership of "CHB". *Cyril Richards Collection*

This unusual scene was recorded by the author on the afternoon of 16th November 1961 and shows the *J. A.P.* aground in the Inner Harbour at Lowestoft. Apparently the vessel was scheduled to be placed on the slipway opposite, but problems arose that ended up with the *J. A. P.* grounding on the foreshore on the south side of Lake Lothing. She was refloated on the next high tide. In the background at the railway sleeper depot, can be seen a former Irish trawler that had been purchased by Claridge Trawlers Ltd. *Copyright Malcolm White*

****
Motor Trawler LT298 *Barton Queen*
Foundered at sea in 1968 with no casualties.

Barton Queen leaves Lowestoft for the fishing grounds.
Copyright Malcolm White

Vessel Details
Built - 1957
Shipbuilder - Richards Ironworks Ltd., Crown Works, Lowestoft. (Yard No. 437)
Official No. - 187020
Call Sign - GXCX
Construction - Steel
Dimensions (feet) - 103.1 x 22.1 x 10.1
Tonnage - 59.0nett / 178.0gross
Engine Type - 6cylinder 440hp Diesel.
Engine Builder - Crossley Brothers Ltd., Openshaw, Manchester

Brief History

1957 Built for Talisman Trawlers Ltd., West Hartlepool and entered service as the side trawler LT298 *Barton Queen*.
1957 Commenced working out of Lowestoft.
1968 *Barton Queen* was abandoned by her crew in the North Sea due to the large amount of water entering the vessel after she had sprung a leak. The trawler later sank.

Loss of the *Barton Queen*

Skipper Michael Reeder of the *Barton Queen* sent out an SOS at about 4.00pm on March 6th 1968 after the trawler sprang a leak which the pumps were unable to cope with. The *Barton Queen* was 150 miles from land and south of the Dogger Bank in mountainous seas, the wind gusting up to 85mph, and blinding snow storms. Fortunately another Lowestoft trawler, the *Wilton Queen* under Skipper Barry Turrell, was about 15 miles away and proceeded to the position where the stricken vessel was, taking almost two hours to get there. After three attempts in the extremely difficult conditions, the *Wilton Queen* managed to pick up the *Barton Queen's* crew of ten from the liferaft they had been in since abandoning their trawler. Another trawler belonging to a company in the same group, the *Ormesby Queen*, stood by the sinking trawler until she disappeared from view.

Skipper Barry Turrell received the Emile Robin award for the rescue of the crew of the *Barton Queen*. This is presented each year by the Shipwrecked Fishermen and Mariners Royal Benevolent Society for the outstanding rescue of the year. (Now presented by the Shipwrecked Mariners' Society).

Note
Both the *Barton Queen* and the *Wilton Queen* were built at Richards shipyard in Lowestoft for Talisman Trawlers Ltd.

An interesting bygone scene showing the *Barton Queen* in the Inner Harbour at Lowestoft. On the far right, where a minesweeper can be seen, is part of the shipyard where she was built.
Copyright John Wells (Wells Photographic)

The *Wilton Queen* picked up the crew of the *Barton Queen* from a liferaft. She is seen here leaving Lowestoft on a fishing trip.
Copyright Malcolm White

****
Motor Fishing Vessel LO496 *William Rhodes Moorhouse*
Sank off Fishguard Harbour in 1968. No casualties.

The William Rhodes Moorhouse off the Welsh coast in 1965.
Copyright Malcolm White

Vessel Details
Built - 1944
Shipbuilder - East Anglian Constructors Ltd., Oulton Broad (Yard No. 336)
Official No. - 166925
Call Sign - MAXE
Construction - Wood
Dimensions (feet) - 93.2 x 22.3 x 9.8
Tonnage - 56.6nett / 112.3gross
Engine Type - 4 cylinder 240hp Diesel
Engine Builder - Crossley Bros. Ltd., Openshaw, Manchester.

Brief History

1943 Ordered on February 18th and intended to be MFV1557, a standard wartime Admiralty motor fishing vessel (MFV).
1944 Ran trials as MFV 1557 on June 29th.
1948 Purchased on January 26th by A. E. Dexter, Torbay Trawlers Ltd., on behalf of Sir Max Aitken M. P.
1948 Ownership details changed to Wellbottom Ltd., Wellbottom Cottage, Gwens Grove, Leatherhead.
1952 Ownership details changed to Wellbottom (Trawlers) Ltd., Leatherhead.
1958 Ownership details changed to Wellbottom Ltd., 83 High Street, Cowes, IOW.
1960 Ownership details changed to Wellbottom Ltd., Leatherhead.
1961 Re-engined with 6cyl 335hp Ruston diesel.
1966 Ownership details changed to Sir Max Aitken.
1966 Sold to P. Wright (Fish Merchant) Ltd., Milford Haven.
1968 Struck a submerged object and sank off Fishguard Harbour.

The loss of the *William Rhodes Moorhouse*

Fishing in Cardigan Bay on Monday April 15th 1968, the *William Rhodes Moorhouse* had trouble with her winch and decided to return to Milford Haven. Whilst returning to port she apparently hit an unknown submerged object and started to leak. The amount of water entering the vessel became serious and a Mayday call was sent out for assistance. Vessels answering the call included LT90 *Dawn Waters*, the Fishguard lifeboat and the tanker *Esso Purfleet*. The skipper and mate stayed on the trawler, but the crew took to their small boat and were picked up by the *Esso Purfleet*.

William Rhodes Moorhouse was taken in tow by the Fishguard lifeboat but she sank 1½ miles from Fishguard Harbour, the skipper and mate being picked up from the water by the lifeboat.

A North Pier view of *William Rhodes Moorhouse* leaving Lowestoft on a fishing trip.
Malcolm White Collection

The Lowestoft registered drifter/trawler *Dawn Waters* which answered the call for assistance from the sinking trawler.
Courtesy Boston Putford Offshore Safety Ltd. (2003)

****
Motor Drifter/Trawler LT671 *Suffolk Warrior*
Sank following a collision in the North Sea in 1969 with no casualties.

The Suffolk Warrior on trials off Lowestoft in 1960 equipped for herring fishing. When she was lost, she was rigged for trawling and is depicted elsewhere in this book in that capacity.
Photographer Ernest Graystone / Copyright Malcolm White

Vessel Details
Built - 1960
Shipbuilder - Richards Ironworks Ltd., Crown Works, Lowestoft. (Yard No. 456)
Official No. - 301535
Call Sign - MCUE
Construction - Steel
Dimensions (feet) - 94.2 x 22.1 x 9.9
Tonnage - 52.48nett / 146.61gross.
Engine Type - 5 cylinder 377hp diesel
Engine Builder - Ruston & Hornsby, Lincoln

Brief History

1960 Built for Small & Co. (Lowestoft) Ltd., Lowestoft and entered service as the drifter/trawler L7671 Suffolk Warrior.
1960 Launched on May 12th 1960,
1960 Ran trials on July 30th and accepted into service.
1964 Under Skipper Ernest Fiske won the Prunier Trophy with 276½ crans of herring which was landed at Great Yarmouth.
1969 Sank in the North Sea in February following a collision with a Dutch trawler.

The loss of the *Suffolk Warrior*

Humber Radio received a call on Saturday February 15th 1969, from the Lowestoft trawler *Suffolk Kinsman* stating that at 6.05am the vessel had received a Mayday (distress) call from the drifter/trawler *Suffolk Warrior* which had been rammed by an unknown vessel about 130 miles from Cromer. She was taking in water and the crew were about to leave the vessel and take to the liferaft. At 7.36am the *Suffolk Kinsman* reported that the crew of the *Suffolk Warrior* were on board the Dutch trawler KW81 *Hendrika Johanna*, which was the other vessel in the collision, and the skipper was on the *Suffolk Kinsman*. It was not advisable to board the *Suffolk Warrior* but the *Suffolk Kinsman* was trying to ascertain the extent of the damage.

Scheveningen Radio received a call at 7.41am from the Dutch trawler involved in the incident which stated:
Approximately 116 miles north by west of Ymuiden had collision with LT671 and hit her aft. She is making water but whole crew of British ship on board KW81. Was willing to take British vessel in tow but, meantime another British ship was asked to do so, they are going to try to go back to LT671. KW81 doesn't need any help but has damage at front.

Humber Radio was called by the *Suffolk Kinsman* at 10.14am with the following message:
Motor fishing vessel *Suffolk Warrior* has sunk in position lat. 52 20N., long. 3 32E. There is debris floating in the area.

Lloyds List published the following on 16th February:
London Feb. 15 - Lowestoft motor fishing vessel *Suffolk Warrior* sank in the North Sea to-day after a collision with Dutch Trawler *Hendrika Johanna* . The collision occurred about 145miles north-east of Lowestoft this morning while the *Suffolk Warrior* was trawling in a south-westerly direction. Despite efforts to get a tow line on board, the *Suffolk Warrior* sank about 10.15am. The skipper and nine crew members got away safely on liferafts and were taken on board the *Hendrika Johanna* but were later transferred to motor trawler *Suffolk Kinsman*. The *Hendrika Johanna* was on a south-westerly course to Katwijk when the collision occurred. The *Suffolk Warrior* was damaged between the bulkhead and the engine room, which was flooded. The crew accommodation flooded immediately after the collision and the vessel began to settle by the stern. Skipper Neil Griffin gave the order to abandon ship and put out a Mayday call. A spokesman for the owners of the *Suffolk Warrior* said that everyone was safe. The *Suffolk Kinsman* is expected to arrive in Lowestoft early tomorrow morning.

Notes
a) Both *Suffolk Warrior* and *Suffolk Kinsman* were owned by Small & Co. (Lowestoft) Ltd. and both were built by Richards Ironworks Ltd., Lowestoft.

b) The Post Office/BT Humber Radio coastal radio station mentioned in the above, closed in June 2000.

Lowestoft Fishing Vessels Remembered - *Section Two*

Two views of the *Suffolk Warrior* leaving Aberdeen for the herring grounds off the Scottish coast.
Copyright Malcolm White

Prior to their vessel sinking, the crew of the *Suffolk Warrior* were taken on board the Dutch trawler that had been involved in the collision. When the Lowestoft trawler *Suffolk Kinsman* (**above**) arrived on the scene the crew were transferred to her for the return to Lowestoft.
Copyright Malcolm White

****

Standby Safety Vessel *Grayfish* (of Lowestoft)
The former Motor Trawler LT361 *Grayfish*

Vessel became a total loss in 1973 after grounding in the Shetlands with no casualties

Newly delivered from her builders, the trawler *Grayfish* leaves Lowestoft on her first fishing trip.
Past Time Maritime Prints

Vessel Details
Built - 1961
Shipbuilder - Richard Dunston Ltd., Thorne
Official No. 302397
Call Sign - MEGL
Construction - Steel
Dimensions (feet) - 94.35 x 21.6 x 8.4
Tonnage - 55nett / 160 gross
Engine Type - 6cylinder 410hp Diesel.
Engine Builder - Ruston & Hornsby, Lincoln.

Brief History

1961 Built for the Huxley Fishing Co. Ltd., Lowestoft and entered service as the side trawler *LT361 Grayfish*.
1972 In use on standby safety vessel duties although technically still a trawler.
1973 Grounded on the Shetlands and vessel became a total loss.

The loss of the *Grayfish*

With poor visibility, a calm sea and wind around Force 1 - 2, the *Grayfish* grounded on the Shetlands at Pundsta Point on December 21st 1973. The Lerwick lifeboat was called out as was the Sandwick Coast Rescue Company which was successful in getting the crew of five ashore safely by breeches buoy. Later the vessel was left high and dry but holed aft. On December 23rd, heavy seas were breaking over the former trawler and by December 31st, it was obvious that the *Grayfish* had suffered badly in the grounding and at the mercy of the rough seas. The damage was considerable and included all the deck gear having being swept away, the wheelhouse had been smashed with parts of it having disappeared and the starboard side and bottom shell plating was extensively holed. Within a short time the vessel broke in two. Little remains of *Grayfish* now but until a few years ago her decaying crumpled rust covered hull (in two sections) could be seen amongst the rocks and rock pools around where she grounded in 1973.

The *Grayfish* approaches the pier heads at Lowestoft after a fishing trip. When she was wrecked she was being used as a standby safety vessel but was essentially a trawler carrying her fishing registration and equipped to return to fishing if required.
Copyright Malcolm White

One of the more recognisable pieces of wreckage from the *Grayfish* in recent years has been the bow section.
Malcolm White Collection

Lowestoft Fishing Vessels Remembered - *Section Two*

****
Motor Trawler LT87 *Jadestar Glory*
Grounded in 1974 on Irish coast with no casualties. Vessel damaged and sold for scrap.

The *Jadestar Glory* leaving Lowestoft for sea when possibly employed on offshore support or survey work.
Copyright Malcolm White

Vessel Details
Built - 1954
Shipbuilder - Cochrane & Sons Ltd. Selby (Yard No. 993)
Official No. - 184002
Call Sign - GSPG
Construction - Steel
Dimensions (feet) - 102.2 x 22.20 x 9.9
Tonnage - 60.20nett / 179.19gross
Engine Type - 6cylinder 350hp Diesel.
Engine Builder - Crossley Brothers Ltd., Openshaw, Manchester

Brief History

1954 Built for Talisman Trawlers Ltd., West Hartlepool.
1954 Launched on May 3rd and ran trials on November 15th.
1954 Registered as LT87 *Ludham Queen* on November 16th, arrived at Lowestoft on the 18th, and sailed on her maiden trip on the 20th.
1967 Ownership transferred to Talisman Trawlers (North Sea) Ltd.
1970 Sold to Henry J. Lamprell, Wareside, Herts and renamed *Jadestar Glory*.
1974 Grounded south of Arklow and sold for scrap.

Loss of the *Jadestar Glory*

Whilst seeking shelter in severe weather the *Jadestar Glory* grounded off Roney Point, County Wexford on January 16th 1974. Skipper Henry John was reported as saying: "We couldn't put the anchor down and were dodging when we struck a submerged rock. She was taking water very fast so we sent out a Mayday message and launched a liferaft which capsized. The trawler's crew prepared to abandon the trawler and board the second liferaft. The gale was about force eleven and the conditions were very bad. After some hours in the liferaft the Arklow lifeboat got to us." Later the trawler refloated and started to drift down on Cahore Point. She went ashore causing her engine room and fish hold to flood. *Jadestar Glory* moved 100 yards up the beach after being abandoned on Cahore Point, and had on board 30 tons of fuel and 20 tons of ice. Skipper John said: "She's driven right inshore, but upright and holed very badly. We are all in pretty good shape." Within a short time of the trawler grounding, a salvage vessel, the *Four Miley* put out to attempt to refloat her, but was herself damaged and returned to Arklow, having left four men on the wrecked trawler to be rescued by helicopter. *Jadestar Glory* was sold to Dublin based Hammond Lane Industries and broken up by that company.

Whilst on charter to an offshore survey company and in the ownership of H. J. Lamprell,
the *Ludham Queen* leaves Great Yarmouth. This scene was recorded before she was renamed.
Copyright Malcolm White

****

Standby Safety Vessel *Kilsyth* (of Lowestoft)
Formerly Motor Trawler LT58 *Boston Pegasus* and PZ375 *Penzance Pegasus*

Scrapped in 1977 at Whitley Bay after grounding there.

Without any fishing gear Kilsyth leaves Lowestoft carrying her Penzance registration.
Copyright Malcolm White

Vessel Details (as a trawler)
Built - 1954
Shipbuilder - Richards Ironworks Ltd., Crown Works, Lowestoft. (Yard No. 421)
Official No. 183999
Call Sign - GSMM
Construction - Steel
Dimensions (feet) - 103.0 x 22.4 x 10.9
Tonnage - 57.24nett / 166.11gross
Engine Type - 6cylinder 370hp Diesel
Engine Builder - Crossley Bros. Ltd., Openshaw, Manchester

Brief History

1954 Built for the Pegasus Trawling Co. Ltd., Fleetwood and launched on July 3rd.
1954 Ran sea trials on September 25th and entered service at Lowestoft as LT58 *Boston Pegasus*.
1954 Landed 2,372 stones of fish from her maiden trip.
1965 Left Lowestoft with over 150 wreaths on board to be placed on the sea where the *Boston Pionair* and her crew were lost.
1968 In service on standby safety duties including being on station adjacent to the oil rig "*Sea Quest*" when she broke adrift on January 15th.
1969 Allocated to various standby safety duties for offshore installations and structures on the Continental Shelf in July.
1971 Sold to Layhill Chartering Co. Ltd., London and identity changed to PZ375 *Penzance Pegasus*.
1973 Sold to Safety Ships Ltd., Aberdeen.
1973 In service at Lowestoft carrying the identity PZ375 *Kilsyth* with all fishing equipment and facilities removed.
1973 In service at Lowestoft carrying the name *Kilsyth* and registered at Lowestoft.
1973 Converted to a standby safety vessel and used in a support role for offshore structures and installations.
1977 Sold to M. Nichols, Shipbreakers, Middlesborough.
1977 Grounded at Whitley Bay and broken up there.

The loss of the *Kilsyth*

Whilst being towed from Aberdeen to a shipbreakers yard at Middlesborough by the tug *Niraround,* the *Kilsyth* grounded on Thursday January 13th 1977 in Whitley Bay.

Due to economic considerations with regard to refloating the vessel, the former trawler was broken up where she lay and within five months there was no trace of her ever being there.

Early morning on the North Pier and the sun is just rising as *Boston Pegasus* approaches the entrance to Lowestoft harbour.
Malcolm White Collection

The *Boston Pegasus* heads for the pier heads at Lowestoft as she leaves on another fishing trip. In the early 1970s, she ceased fishing and became the *Penzance Pegasus* and later *Kilsyth*.
Malcolm White Collection

****
Motor Stern Trawler LT328 *Boston Sea Ranger*
Capsized and sank in 1977 with the loss of five crew members

The Boston Sea Ranger leaves Lowestoft on a North Sea fishing trip.
Photographer Ernest Graystone / Copyright Malcolm White

Vessel Details
Year Built - 1976
Shipbuilder(s) - J. R. Hepworth & Co. (Hull) Ltd., Paull
(Completed by Cochrane & Sons Ltd., Selby)
Official No. 376317
Call Sign - GVUV
Construction - Steel
Dimensions (feet) - 84.5 x 24.10 x 11.4
Tonnage - 58.64nett / 171.05gross
Engine Type - 8cylinder 700hp Diesel.
Engine Builder - Mirrlees Blackstone (Stamford) Ltd., Stamford.

Brief History

1976 Built for the Boston Deep Sea Fisheries Ltd., Hull and launched on August 26th.
1976 Entered service at Lowestoft as the stern trawler LT328 *Boston Sea Ranger*.
1976 Skipper Lace took command of the *Boston Sea Ranger* from new having previously been skipper of the *Boston Viking*. He attended a course at Hull on midwater fishing techniques before taking over the new trawler.
1976 Sailed on first fishing trip (not maiden trip) on December 17th with Skipper Ian Lace in charge.
1976 Landed 61 kits at Lowestoft worth £2,162 on December 23rd.
1977 Sank off Lands End in December resulting in the loss of five crewmen.

The loss of the *Boston Sea Ranger*

The stern trawler *Boston Sea Ranger*, which had an eight man crew, capsized and sank 4.6 miles off Land's End at about 1.00am on December 5th 1977. She had been fishing for mackerel on the Epson Shoal. Three crewmen lost their lives, two others were reported as missing, and there were three survivors. The survivors had been picked up from two liferafts by the Sennen Cove lifeboat at approximately 2.30am and were then transferred to the Hull stern trawler *Arctic Buccaneer*. Of the five who were lost, three were found in the water and were taken on board the *Arctic Buccaneer*. One was already dead and the other two were airlifted off the trawler by helicopter, however one died on the way to Culdrose naval air station and the other died in the base hospital about one hour after being admitted. The extensive search for the two missing crew members was called off at 9.30am by the Lands End headquarters of HM Coastguard at St. Just, after any hope of finding them alive vanished. Involved in the search had been three helicopters from RNAS Culdrose, a Nimrod aircraft from RAF St. Mawgen, the Penlee and Sennen Cove lifeboats, and nine fishing vessels including the *Arctic Buccaneer* and the *St. Benedict* which had both been anchored in Sennen Cove. After the search had been called off, a team of men were posted on the cliff top at Gwennap Head in case the bodies of the two missing crewmen were washed up.

The survivors from the *Boston Sea Ranger* were the skipper, Mr. Ian Lace of Glebe Close, Lowestoft; the mate, Mr. Michael Reynolds of Dedham Drive, Lowestoft and the third hand Mr. Raymond Palmer of Victoria Street, Southwold. Those who lost their lives as a result of the trawler capsizing were named as Mr. J. S. Clark, of Love Road, Lowestoft and Mr. A. H. Smith of Austin Road, Cobholm, Great Yarmouth. The name of the crew member who died in hospital was announced during the afternoon of December 5th as Mr. T. Switzer, of Wainiford Road, Pennington, Hants. Details of the two missing crewmen were announced several hours after the search had been called off; they were named as Mr. Michael Studd of Wissett Way, Lowestoft and Mr. Le-Poideven, of Southwold Road, Wrentham.

The news of the tragedy was broken to relatives by Mr. Ben Green, Senior Superintendent of the Royal National Mission to Deep Sea Fishermen (RNMDSF), and the Port Missionary, the Rev. Malcolm Pears. A memorial service for the crew members who died in the *Boston Sea Ranger* tragedy was held at the Bethel at 3.00pm on Sunday January 8th 1978. The service was conducted by Mr. Ben Green and the Rev. Malcolm Pears. The address was given by the Bishop of Norwich.

An appeal launched by Mr. Nicholas Brighouse, Chairman of Waveney District Council for the dependants of those lost at sea in the *Boston Sea Ranger* raised more than £12,000 and a similar appeal in Penzance had a target of £3,000 but the money collected exceeded this. All the money collected was absorbed into a central fund to avoid administration problems.

Lloyds List - Sequence of Events
Published Tuesday December 6th 1977

Land's End Coastguard, Dec 5
Red flare sighted from Gwennap Head at 0106, GMT by Coastguard and acknowledged by white star. Sennen Cove Lifeboat advised to launch. Gwennap Head making preliminary Pan (urgency) broadcast.

Land's End Radio, Dec 5
Ref red flares, motor stern trawler *Boston Sea Ranger* sank in position 180 deg. true, two miles Gwennap Head, four crew still missing. Sennen Cove lifeboat and several trawlers searching. Nimrod and helicopter proceeding.

Land's End Coastguard, Dec 5
Boston Sea Ranger, with eight crew, fishing the Epson Shoal, 166 deg Gwennap Head 4.6miles, capsized. Present weather, wind south force 5 (fresh breeze), sea slight, visibility eight miles. Three survivors picked up from two liferafts by lifeboat at 0233hrs. and transferred to motor stern trawler *Arctic Buccaneer*. Other trawlers assisting in search. One man recovered from water unconscious and one body recovered. Three crewmen still missing. Established red flares fired from liferaft.

Land's End Coastguard, Dec 5 (A second message)
Three crewmen picked up from liferafts all safe and well on board *Arctic Buccaneer* and will be landed at Newlyn. Two men, one unconscious and one believed dead, recovered and transferred to Culdrose by helicopter, also one body recovered by helicopter. Only two liferafts launched, both have been recovered.

Land's End Radio, Dec 5
Boston Sea Ranger. Search called off at 0930, GMT. Nothing further found, two crew still missing. Cancel broadcast.

London, Dec 5
Three men were dead and two feared dead after their vessel, *Boston Sea Ranger* capsized and sank five miles off Land's End early today. Three survivors, plus two bodies and an unconscious crew member who died later, were picked up in a rescue operation which involved other trawlers, lifeboats and helicopters. Amongst those rescued was the skipper, Mr. Ian Lace, who reported that a massive wave struck the vessels stern, flooding one of the main fish storage compartments. The vessel capsized soon after and two liferafts were launched.

A summary of the account given to a local newspaper by Skipper Lace following the loss of the *Boston Sea Ranger*

Skipper Lace said that the crew were getting in the remainder of a catch of mackerel with already about 50 tons of fish in the fish room, when a very heavy swell ran over the stern of the trawler and filled the afterdeck. This resulted in water pouring into the port fishroom but before the hatches were clamped down another heavy swell came aboard and more water poured down below. The result was that the *Boston Sea Ranger* took a list to port, and as a precaution, Skipper Lace told the crew to get on deck and put their lifejackets on. There seemed no real danger, but also as a precaution, he told the mate to get the liferafts ready. However the position worsened when the engineer reported that because of the list, he could get no suction on the pumps and there was no way of clearing the water. After telling the crew members to get their own lifejackets on, he said he went to his berth to get his own. To get to his berth he passed through the engine room and coming back he found that he was actually walking on the side of the ship. Skipper Lace thought that the list was 45 degrees or more. By the time he was back on deck, the list was critical and within a very short time the trawler rolled over and sank. He recalled how he went down with the trawler, part of the superstructure of the ship hitting him as it sank, but somehow, still holding his lifejacket, he became free and found himself on the surface. Having inflated automatically, a liferaft from the sunken trawler came to the surface about 25 yards from where Skipper Lace was. He managed to swim to it and get on board despite the liferaft being swamped. He then fired off some flares. In the other liferaft, made ready for launching before the trawler sank, were two members of the crew also firing flares. Skipper Lace was picked up by the Sennen Cove lifeboat about two hours after the *Boston Sea Ranger* sank and was taken to the Hull trawler *Arctic Buccaneer*. Although cold and exhausted, Skipper Lace said he was terribly worried about the rest of the crew, and insisted on being put on one of the small boats which were launched from the *Arctic Buccaneer* and which picked up two men, Tony Smith and John Clark. When recovered from the sea, Tony Smith was certainly alive and it was thought that John Clark may have been. He was later told that Mr. Smith had passed away, and Mr. Clark was already dead when taken from the sea. Skipper Lace said in his opinion it was the cold and exposure that had killed them and added that he would like to thank the two Hull trawlers, the lifeboat and helicopter crews, the people of Penzance, the coastguards and all who helped in any way.

The R.N.L.I. and R.N.A.S. Culdrose accounts of the events following the sinking of the *Boston Sea Ranger*

Captain Ewan Watson, secretary of Sennen branch of the R.N.L.I. stated that the coxswain of the lifeboat saw a red flare ahead of the boat when they arrived on the scene. They found a liferaft with two survivors inside and took them on board. Another survivor, believed to be the trawler's skipper, was found in a second liferaft a few minutes later. "The three men were very wet and cold so they were transferred to the Hull trawler *Arctic Buccaneer*.
The skipper of the *Boston Sea Ranger* was particularly anxious to get on board the Hull trawler so he could use the trawler's telephone to find out if the rest of the crew had been picked up," said Captain Watson.

The first Sea King helicopter to leave RNAS Culdrose was piloted by Lt. Nigel Arnall-Culliford who later said at the base that they had picked up two of the five men aboard the *Arctic Buccaneer* as they were in a critical condition: "The winchman went down and picked up the two men, who were on stretchers, from the forecastle of the *Arctic Buccaneer*. One of them died on the way to Culdrose and the other in the base hospital," he said. Lt. Arnall-Culliford also said there was a fairly strong swell at the time and the wind was gusting up to 25knots. Another Sea King from Culdrose picked up a further body and in all the helicopters were searching for four hours. They were relieved by a Wessex helicopter from Culdrose which searched for two hours before the search was called off.

Court of Inquiry into the loss of the *Boston Sea Ranger*

A Court of Inquiry into the loss of the *Boston Sea Ranger*, commenced on July 9th 1979 at the Great Yarmouth Masonic Hall with Mr. Gerald Darling Q.C. as the chairman. The Department of Trade (DOT) put forward 57 questions requiring answers by the court. The findings of the inquiry included a statement about how Boston Deep Sea Fisheries, the owners of the *Boston Sea Ranger*, had been engaged in a new venture when they turned to mackerel fishing. It was pointed out that a trawler mackerel fishing could catch in minutes weights of fish that in the North Sea whilst trawling for white fish, would take a month. Instead of the catch being iced and shelved as in the North Sea operations, a large catch of mackerel would be a fluid and slippery mass. The trawler's owners had sought advice about sending their vessels on the new venture from the builders of the *Boston Sea Ranger* and her sister ships, and had prepared special instructions for their skippers based on the advice from the builders. The court considered the instructions were a "model of clarity." However, in the light of hindsight the court suggested that the instructions could have been improved by one further sentence to explain the underlying purpose of the instructions and the grave peril which would result from disobedience. The court commented that: "We feel, however, that the owners failed (a) to be sufficiently positive in enforcing their instructions and ensuring that they were understood, (b) to take every step to ensure that the *Boston Sea Ranger* was properly fitted out for bulk mackerel fishing when she reverted to that mode of fishing early in November 1977, and (c) to remind skippers at that time that special instructions were still in force." For these failures, which they found were contributory causes of the *Boston Sea Ranger's* loss, the court felt bound to censure Boston Deep Sea Fisheries. They felt that the company might have been well advised to consider carefully what qualifications a manager in the fishing industry should have, if he was to carry out all his duties effectively and whether the level of knowledge of stability in their management team at the time of the casualty was really sufficient.

Boston Deep Sea Fisheries admitted to the overloading of the trawler *Boston Sea Knight* not long after the loss of her sister ship. The report said that this had came to light during the investigation preceding the inquiry and "came as something of a shock to the court."

Court of Inquiry into the loss of the *Boston Sea Ranger* (continued from previous page)

Mr. Lace had acknowledged through his counsel that he had failed in his duty as a skipper in a number of respects. Most of the admitted failures really added up to neglect to comply with the owners' special instructions for mackerel fishing. The court had already considered these instructions and, subject to the observations they had made, were entirely adequate. Failure to comply with them was obviously the principal cause of the loss of the trawler. Their link with stability was clearly indicated by the governing phase, "so that the vessel meets the acceptable stability criteria." The inquiry considered that the ice scuttles should not have been used for loading fish in the prevailing weather conditions, and that the listing of the trawler was not only unnecessary, but was particularly dangerous as it had the effect of listing the vessel when she was already deep draughted, increasing her draught aft and creating a further free surface area. If the vessel had to be listed fuel oil transfer should have been employed. Another point in the report concerned the manning of the bridge and stated that it was basic that the bridge must be manned at all times when the vessel was under way. The bridge of the *Boston Sea Ranger* was very well laid out and equipped to enable the skipper to keep watch and to control the fishing.

Finally the report stated that a skipper should always insist on being informed of the state of his fuel tanks on sailing.

In conclusion the report stated: "Having carefully considered the demeanour and attitude of Skipper Lace, the evidence of what he did while exercising command and the mitigating factors - his frank admissions, the respects in which the owners failed in their duties and the period of time which has elapsed since the casualty - we nevertheless cannot overlook his very serious failures in this case."

The outcome of the Court of Inquiry was that the skipper of the trawler had his skipper's certificate suspended for 18 months, however, Mr. Lace was granted a temporary certificate as a mate. The owners of the trawler were ordered to pay £1,000 towards the cost of the inquiry. The court found that the loss of the trawler was "partly caused or contributed to by the wrongful act or default by the company or Mr. Lace."

To the questions raised by the DOT, "Was the loss of any of her officers and crew caused or contributed to by the wrongful act of any person or persons?" - the inquiry answered "no."

Memorial Service to the Men who lost their lives on the

BOSTON SEA RANGER

on Monday 5th December 1977

Held in

Lowestoft Sailors and Fishermens Bethel

Battery Green Road

Sunday 8th January 1978 at 3.00 p.m.

J. S. CLARKE DECK HAND,   M. D. STUDD DECK HAND

E. H. Le-POIDEVEN CHIEF ENGINEER   A. H. SMITH COOK

T. SWITZER DECK HAND

The Chairman and members of the Waveney District Council will be in attendance.

The front cover of the Order of Service used at the Bethel on Sunday January 8th 1978. .
(Reduced in size for inclusion in this book).
Malcolm White Collection

Mr. Raymond Palmer
Third Hand on the *Boston Sea Ranger*

Included in the Lowestoft Journal of July 26th 2013 was a report of the death, at the age of 81, of Mr. Raymond Palmer. Mr. Palmer was awarded the Royal Humane Society bronze medal for bravery in 1978 after he gave his lifejacket to the cook, Tony Smith, as the *Boston Sea Ranger* sank. Mr. Palmer was a strong swimmer and was able to swim to a liferaft and became one of the three survivors when the trawler sank off Cornwall. Mr. Smith was a non swimmer and had only partial use of one arm.

Southwold born Mr. Palmer was also made a Member of the Silver Spur by the Order of the Knights of the Round Table of King Arthur's Court at Plymouth for his chivalrous deed. He also received a framed copy of a council resolution recording his bravery from Southwold Town Council.

Mr. Palmer sailed out of Lowestoft on trawlers owned by Boston Deep Sea Fisheries for many years and was well known in the fishing community.

Top - The *Boston Sea Knight* was mentioned at the inquiry due to her being found to be overloaded after the *Boston Sea Ranger* capsized. *Photographer Ernest Graystone / Copyright Malcolm White*
Bottom - The *Boston Sea Ranger* heads for the harbour entrance at Lowestoft. *Photographer Ernest Graystone / Copyright Malcolm White*

****
Motor Trawler LT132 *St. Luke*
Sank following an explosion at sea in 1978 with no casualties

The impressive size of this distant water trawler is well illustrated here as the *St. Luke* enters Lowestoft harbour at the end of another fishing trip.
Copyright Malcolm. White

Vessel Details
Built - 1961
Shipbuilder - Hall, Russell & Co. Ltd., Aberdeen (Yard No. 897)
Official No. 303204
Call Sign - GHPX
Construction - Steel
Dimensions (feet) - 138 x 28.1 x 14
Tonnage - 127nett / 391gross
Engine Type - 7cylinder 1022hp Diesel.
Engine Builder - Mirrlees, Bickerton & Day Ltd. Stockport, England

Brief History

1961 Built for Parbel-Smith Ltd., Aberdeen and entered service as A574 *Admiral Burnett*
1963 Sold to Mannofield Fishing Co. Ltd., Aberdeen.
1966 Sold to St. Andrews Steam Fishing Co. Ltd., Hull.
1968 Ownership passed to Boston Deep Sea Fisheries Ltd., Hull and the trawler's identity changed to FD14 *Boston Lightning*.
1976 Sold to Dagon Fishing Co. Ltd., Lowestoft.
1976 Arrived at Lowestoft on December 4th.
1977 Identity changed briefly to LT132 *Boston Lighning* before receiving her new name of *St. Luke*.
1978 Sank in the North Sea following an explosion near the trawler whilst the nets were being hauled.

The loss of the *St. Luke*

On May 18th 1978, the crew of eleven abandoned the *St. Luke* as she sank following an explosion that occurred whilst the nets were being hauled approximately 160 miles off the Yorkshire coast.

It was presumed that a mine or similar explosive device had been caught in the trawl and detonated either on the sea bed or when it was in close proximity to the trawler.

Still carrying her previous name but not her old registration, *Boston Lightning* leaves her new home port of Lowestoft for the fishing grounds. At that time (1977) the trawler was in the ownership of the Dagon Fishing Co. Ltd., a company within the Colne Group, a major Lowestoft based fishing and shipping concern.
Copyright Malcolm White

Lowestoft Fishing Vessels Remembered - Section Two

****
Standby Safety Vessel *Cuttlefish* (of Lowestoft)
The former Motor Trawler LT65 *Cuttlefish*

Vessel sank after grounding on the Haisborough Sands in 1981 with no casualties.

The former trawler *Cuttlefish* leaves Lowestoft for another spell of standby safety duty in the southern North Sea.
Copyright Malcolm White

Vessel Details (as a trawler)
Built - 1959
Shipbuilder - Richard Dunston Ltd., Thorne (Yard No. 993)
Official No. 301513
Call Sign - GDLE
Construction - Steel
Dimensions (feet) - 94.5 x 21.4 x 8.4
Tonnage - 54.15nett / 152.9gross
Engine Type - 6cylinder 360hp Diesel.
Engine Builder - Ruston & Hornsby, Lincoln.

Brief History

1958 Launched on September 27th for Claridge Trawlers Ltd., Lowestoft.
1959 Registered on April 2nd and entered service as the side trawler LT65 *Cuttlefish*.
1960 Slightly damaged at sea in June after being in collision with the trawler *Warbler*.
1969 Slightly damaged in a collision on April 7th with the trawler *Boston Trident*.
1971 Occasionally in use on standby safety vessel duties although technically still a trawler.
1974 On December 5th picked up five of the crew of the supply ship *Tropic Shore* from a liferaft after she had collided with the drilling rig *Britannia* 40 miles north east of Cromer. Four other crew members were picked up by a Bristow Helicopter from Yarmouth just seconds before the *Tropic Shore* rolled over and sank.
1975 No longer fishing and registry closed in December.
1976 Fully converted for use as a standby safety vessel (100 survivor class) and used to support offshore operations.
1981 Grounded on Haisborough Sands and later sank.

The loss of the *Cuttlefish*

On Monday November 30th 1981, the former trawler *Cuttlefish* grounded in rough seas on Haisborough Sands. There were no casualties, the six men on board being taken off the vessel by helicopter and lifeboat. The next day a representative of the owners said that helicopters had located two liferafts, and the fact that these were inflated indicated that the *Cuttlefish* was under water. Oil had also been seen coming to the surface presumably from the tanks of the vessel. "We had two of our vessels there till mid-afternoon and nothing else was seen," said the spokesman. It was stated that inquiries into the sinking were being a carried out by the owners and the Department of Trade and Industry.

From 1959 until 1975 the *Cuttlefish* served as a trawler, the role in which we see her here leaving Lowestoft on a fishing trip.
Malcolm White Collection

****

Standby Safety Vessel *Spearfish* (of Lowestoft)
The former Motor Trawler LT232 *Spearfish*
Deliberately sunk in 1983 after becoming a hazard.

After conversion to a safety standby vessel, the *Spearfish* leaves Lowestoft
to take up station near an offshore rig or gas production platform.
Copyright Malcolm White

Vessel Details (as a trawler)
Year Built - 1956
Shipbuilder - Richard Dunston Ltd., Thorne (Yard No. T927)
Official No. 187009
Call Sign - GVGT
Construction - Steel
Dimensions (feet) - 94.5 x 21.4 x 8.4
Tonnage - 49nett / 151gross
Engine Type - 6cylinder 360hp Diesel.
Engine Builder - Ruston & Hornsby, Lincoln

Brief History

1956 Built for Claridge Trawlers Ltd. Lowestoft and entered service as the side trawler LT232 *Spearfish*.
1971 In use on standby safety vessel duties although technically still a trawler.
1976 Fully converted for use as a standby safety vessel (100 survivor class) and used to support offshore operations.
1982 Ownership of the vessel changed to Colne Shipping Co. Ltd., Lowestoft
1983 Partially sank on June 29th following a collision in the English Channel with a drilling rig.
1983 As a danger to shipping, the vessel was sunk by gunfire by HMS *Tartar*.

The loss of the *Spearfish*

On June 29th 1983, the standby safety vessel *Spearfish* collided with the drilling rig *Penrod 85* which was drilling a wildcat well about 17 miles south of St. Catherines Point on the Isle of Wight. Apparently dragged by strong currents, the *Spearfish* hit one of the legs of the drilling rig and became tangled in the rig's structure. Over an hour was spent in freeing the former trawler from the rig by which time she was badly damaged. The *Spearfish* was towed away from *Penrod 85* by the standby safety vessel *St. Lucia* and the supply ship *Leam Texas*. By this time only the bow of the *Spearfish* was visible, kept afloat by trapped air. The *Spearfish* was considered a hazard to shipping by the Queens Harbour Master at Portsmouth and after contacting Colne Shipping, arrangements were made for the frigate HMS *Tartar* (F133) to sink the *Spearfish* by gunfire well away from the drilling rig, and restricted and sensitive areas. The crew of six had all been taken off the *Spearfish* by the helicopter from HMS *Tartar* as soon as it was considered unsafe for them to stay on the former trawler, all were unhurt in the rescue.

Right - Still essentially a trawler but carrying out the duties of a standby safety vessel, the *Spearfish* is seen on station near the *Transocean 11* drilling rig while a crew change for rig workers takes place.

Photographer Robert Lewis
Copyright Malcolm White

****
Standby Safety Vessel *Margaret Christina* (of Lowestoft)
Formerly motor trawler *LT331 Margaret Christina*
Sank at sea in 1983 with no casualties.

Left - The *Margaret Christina* as a standby safety vessel, the role that she was undertaking when she sank.
Right - Before conversion and as originally built, the trawler LT331 *Margaret Christina*
Both Copyright Malcolm White

Vessel Details (as a trawler)
Year Built - 1960
Shipbuilder - Richards Ironworks Ltd., Lowestoft (Yard No. 459)
Official No. 302388
Call Sign - GHDY
Construction - Steel
Dimensions (feet) - 92.5 x 22.3 x 9.75
Tonnage - 48nett/ 137gross
Engine Type - 6cylinder 360hp Diesel.
Engine Builder - Ruston & Hornsby, Lincoln.

Brief History

1960 Built for East Anglian Ice & Cold Storage Co. Ltd. and entered service as the side trawler LT331 *Margaret Christina*
1969 Ownership transferred to Small & Co. (Lowestoft) Ltd.
1970 Left Lowestoft on April 30th after being sold to Southern Marine, Malahide, ROI.
1970 Fishing registration cancelled and vessel registered at Dublin.
1971 Sold to Putford Enterprises Ltd., and arrived back at Lowestoft on December 10th.
1971 Allocated fishing registration LT331.
1972 In use as standby safety vessel and used to provide support for offshore installations and structures.
1975 On December 13th, under Skipper Arthur Keable, rescued the crew of the Hull tug *Norman* in gale force winds near the West Sole gas field. Skipper Keable received the Emile Robin award for this incident. This is presented annually by the Shipwrecked Fishermen and and Mariners Royal Benevolent Society for an outstanding rescue. He also received an award from the Department of Trade for the same rescue.
1976 On March 8th, picked up the passengers and crew of a Wessex helicopter that had gone down in the North Sea off the Yorkshire coast. In total, 14 persons were recovered from the North Sea in this incident.
1977 On March 28th, picked up five survivors from the Grimsby trawler *Sioux* that had sunk in stormy seas off the Humber estuary. The skipper of the *Sioux* was unfortunately lost.
1983 Developed a leak and sank near the Leman Bank in the North Sea whilst on standby safety duty.
1983 Vessel raised and taken to Holland for scrapping.

The loss of the *Margaret Christina*

On September 12th 1983, the *Margaret Christina* was at her allocated standby position near the Leman Bank when she developed a serious leak and her crew of five took to a liferaft. The crew were picked up by an inflatable from the Lowestoft standby safety vessel *Southleigh* whilst the skipper was picked up by the Danish tug *Svitzer Jarl*. The skipper was transferred to the *Southleigh* and the tug then attempted to tow the *Margaret Christina,* but within an hour the attempt to tow the sinking vessel had to be abandoned as she sank. Due to the wreck being approximately 300 metres from a gas pipe line, the *Margaret Christina* was later raised by the sheerlegs pontoon *Taklift 4* and taken to Holland. The Dutch owned *Taklift 4* could lift 1600 tons and at the time was considered one of the largest of her type in the world. She took the wreck to Rotterdam arriving there on October 22nd, and the *Margaret Christina* was later scrapped there.

Note
The *Southleigh* was also owned by Putford Enterprises Ltd. and built at Richards Ironworks Ltd. in Lowestoft.

The standby safety vessel *Southleigh* which was involved in saving the crew of the *Margaret Christina*. She was originally the Lowestoft drifter/trawler *Young Duke*.
Copyright Malcolm White

****

Standby Safety Vessel *Abaco* (of Lowestoft)
Formerly Motor Trawler GY644 *Judaean*
Caught fire and badly damaged at sea in 1984 with no casualties.

Left - The standby safety vessel *Abaco* leaves Lowestoft to take up station near an offshore structure or installation.
Right - The *Abaco* was built as the Grimsby trawler GY644 *Judaean*.
Both photographs Copyright Malcolm White

Vessel Details (as in 1984)
Built - 1960
Shipbuilder - Cochrane & Sons Ltd., Selby. (Yard No. 1449)
Official No. 301837
Call Sign - GGHK
Construction - Steel
Dimensions (feet) - 119.50 x 25.00 x 11.9
Tonnage - 86nett / 272gross
Engine Type - 5cylinder 790hp Diesel.
Engine Builder - British Polar Engines Ltd., Glasgow.

Brief History

1961 Built for Sir Thomas Robinson & Sons (GY) Ltd., Grimsby and entered service as the side trawler GY644 *Judaean*.
1976 Sold to Dagon Fishing Co. Ltd., Lowestoft (a Colne Group company).
1976 Arrived at Lowestoft on November 25th.
1977 Converted to a standby safety vessel and renamed *Abaco* with Lowestoft as her port of registry. Vessel used to provide safety services to offshore structures and installations.
1982 Ownership of the vessel changed to Colne Shipping Co. Ltd., Lowestoft.
1984 Caught fire on July 17th in the North Sea, fire extinguished and vessel towed to Lowestoft.
1985 Sold for scrapping at Gravesend.
1985 Left Lowestoft on November 16th.

The loss of the *Abaco*

Whilst off the Humber on July 17th 1984, the standby safety vessel *Abaco* caught fire and suffered severe damage before the fire was extinguished. The crew took to the liferaft and were picked up by a Danish trawler which then transferred the crew to the Lowestoft standby safety vessel *Blackburn Rovers*. *Abaco* was towed by the *Blackburn Rovers* back to Lowestoft where upon arrival, the tug *Ala* brought her into harbour. Much of her superstructure, afterdecks and plates were scorched, buckled and bent, and the wheelhouse was sagging and melted. In March 1985, *Abaco* was declared a total loss, and in November 1985, she was towed by the tug *Eugenio* to the yard of shipbreaker Henderson & Morez Ltd., at Gravesend, arriving there on November 17th.

After the fire the standby safety vessel *Blackburn Rovers* (**above**) towed the *Abaco* back to her home port.
Copyright Malcolm White

The fire damage *Abaco* after she had been towed back to Lowestoft.
Copyright PLRS

Lowestoft Fishing Vessels Remembered - *Section Two*

****

Standby Safety Vessel *Bahama* (of Lowestoft)
Formerly Motor Trawler LT142 *Bahama*
Scrapped in 1986 on Aldeburgh Beach after grounding there.

Left - The trawler LT142 *Bahama* leaves Lowestoft on a fishing trip. *Malcolm White Collection*
Right - The standby safety vessel *Bahama* arrives back at her home port after a spell of standby duty adjacent to a offshore rig or platform. *Copyright Malcolm White*

Vessel Details (as in 1985)
Year Built - 1957
Shipbuilder - Henry Scarr Ltd., Hessle (Yard No. 749)
Note - The Henry Scarr shipyard was acquired in 1932 by Richard Dunston Ltd. but shipbuilding
at the Hessle yard continued under the Henry Scarr name until the early 1960s.
Official No. 187023
Call Sign - MXYL
Construction - Steel
Dimensions (feet) - 106.0 x 23.15 x 9.1
Tonnage - 67nett / 204gross
Engine Type - 6cylinder 446hp Diesel.
Engine Builder - Ruston & Hornsby Ltd., Lincoln

Brief History

1957 Built for the Colne Fishing Co. Ltd., Lowestoft and entered service as the side trawler LT142 *Bahama*.
1976 Fully converted to a standby safety vessel and used to provide support for offshore installations and structures.
1982 Ownership of the vessel changed to Colne Shipping Co. Ltd., Lowestoft.
1986 Grounded on the beach at Aldeburgh and, due to sustaining substantial hull damage, was scrapped there.

The loss of the *Bahama*

On June 20th 1986, the *Bahama* left Lowestoft with the standby safety vessel *Kennedy* for the shipbreakers yard of G. T. Services Ltd., at Barking where both vessels were scheduled to be scrapped. The *Kennedy* was towing the *Bahama* and at about 7.45am off Aldeburgh in force 7 winds, the tow rope parted with the result that the *Bahama* was blown onto the beach hitting some steel groynes. Her hull was holed in several places and after a number of unsuccessful salvage attempts she was sold for scrap and broken up on the beach.

Note

The *Kennedy*, was originally the Fleetwood trawler FD139 *Boston Britannia*. She was purchased by the Colne Fishing Co. Ltd. and arrived at Lowestoft in 1976 where she was fully converted into a standby safety vessel.

The *Bahama* ashore on the beach at Aldeburgh on June 22nd 1986. Once the tow parted, sea conditions and the onshore wind drove the stranded former trawler higher up the beach.
Courtesy Colne Shipping Ltd. (2000)

The vessel towing the *Bahama* when the tow parted was the larger standby vessel *Kennedy*. This impressive former distant water trawler is seen here leaving Lowestoft to take up station adjacent to an offshore installation or platform.
Copyright Malcolm White

Lowestoft Fishing Vessels Remembered - Section Two

****

Standby Safety Vessel *St. Mark* (of Lowestoft)
Former Motor Trawler LT327 *St. Mark*

Sank following a collision at sea in 1990 with no casualties.

Before her conversion to a standby safety vessel, LT327 *St. Mark* heads out of Lowestoft for the fishing grounds.
Copyright Malcolm White

Vessel Details (as in 1985)
Built - 1960
Shipbuilder - J. Lewis & Sons Ltd., Aberdeen
Official No. 302523
Call Sign - GHFA
Construction - Steel
Dimensions (feet) - 139.9 x 28.5 x 13.9
Tonnage - 142nett / 407gross
Engine Type - 6cylinder 1230hp Diesel.
Engine Builder - British Polar Engines Ltd., Helen Street, Glasgow.

Brief History

1960 Built for the Iago Steam Fishing Co. Ltd., Fleetwood and entered service as the side trawler LO33 *Captain Foley*
1972 Identity changed to GY210 *Boston Tristar* following the merging of Iago Steam Fishing Co. Ltd. with Boston Deep Sea Fisheries Ltd.
1976 Sold in July to the Colne Fishing Co. Ltd., Lowestoft and vessel repainted in Colne Group colours.
1976 Identity changed to LT327 *St. Mark* in October.
1980 Fully converted by late June to become a standby safety vessel (250 survivor class) for use in providing safety services to offshore structures and installations. Her first assignment was to standby a drilling ship 300miles off the west coast of Scotland in the Rockall Trough area.
1982 Ownership of the vessel changed to Colne Shipping Co. Ltd., Lowestoft
1990 Sank off the North Norfolk Coast following a collision.
2012 Video of the decaying remains of the *St. Mark* was released on the internet in scenes recorded by a team of divers.

The loss of the *St. Mark*

The *St. Mark* sank following a collision with the tug *Vikingbank* off Cromer on August 6th 1990. With the former trawler sinking, the crew of ten took to the liferafts and were soon picked up by the 197ft. supply/support ship *Suffolk Mariner*. A Wessex helicopter from RAF Coltishall was dispatched to rendezvous with the *Suffolk Mariner*, which had been four miles away when the collision occurred. The helicopter picked up eight survivors from the deck of the *Suffolk Mariner* and took them, with two others already rescued, directly to the James Paget Hospital at Gorleston for a check up.

It was reported that the *St. Mark* sank in 85ft. of water and that the Cromer lifeboat, with Coxswain Richard Davies at the helm, had stood by the sinking vessel for a time after the helicopter had left the scene. The lifeboat recovered the two drifting and empty liferafts used by the crew when they abandoned the *St. Mark*. The tug *Vikingbank* was towing a 100 metre long barge destined for the nuclear power station at Sizewell which is south of Southwold. Apparently she did not suffer any great damage from the collision and continued on her way to Sizewell with the barge.

Waiting in the bridge channel at Lowestoft the standby safety vessel *St. Mark*, makes an imposing sight in the morning sunshine.
Photographer Ernest Graystone / Copyright Malcolm White

The last few minutes of the *St. Mark* as she slips beneath the waves off the North Norfolk coast.
Courtesy Cromer RNLI (2000)

****
Standby Safety Vessel *St. Martin* (of Lowestoft)
Formerly Motor Trawler LT376 *St. Martin*

Sank at sea in 1991 with no casualties.

The standby safety vessel *St. Martin* off Lowestoft and heading for the harbour entrance.
Copyright Malcolm White

Vessel Details (as in 1985)

Built - 1961
Shipbuilder - Henry Scarr Ltd., Hessle (Yard No. 773)
Note - The Henry Scarr shipyard was acquired in 1932 by Richard Dunston Ltd. but shipbuilding at the Hessle yard continued under the Henry Scarr name until the early 1960s.
Official No. 302406
Call Sign - GHTY
Construction - Steel
Dimensions (feet) - 113.7 x 25.7 x 11.15
Tonnage - 75nett / 234gross
Engine Type - 6cylinder 440hp Diesel
Engine Builder - Ruston & Hornsby, Lincoln

Brief History

1961 Built for the Colne Fishing Co. Ltd., Lowestoft and entered service as the side trawler LT376 *St. Martin*.

1965 Under Skipper Harry Blowers towed for 22 hours in extreme conditions the Lowestoft trawler *Bermuda* which had engine trouble, arriving back at Lowestoft on November 3rd.

1965 Under Skipper Harry Blowers towed for 56 hours in very heavy seas the Lowestoft trawler *Kingfish* which had engine trouble, arriving back at Lowestoft on December 2nd.

1966 Under Skipper Ernest Peek on the September 5th picked up the sole survivor from the German submarine *Hai* in the area of Clay Deeps about 150miles north east of Lowestoft.

1978 Converted to a standby safety vessel and used to provide safety services to offshore structures.

1982 Ownership of the vessel changed to Colne Shipping Co. Ltd., Lowestoft.

1991 Sank in the North Sea after she sprang a leak.

Note - The trawlers *St. Martin*, *Bermuda* and *Kingfish* were all owned by companies within the Colne Group.

The loss of the *St. Martin*

At 1412hrs on the January 10th 1991 the *St. Martin* reported that she required immediate assistance whilst about 80 miles off the Lincolnshire coast. It was arranged for the RAF helicopter "Rescue 125" to respond to the call with an estimated time of arrival of 1600hrs. Due to the deteriorating situation with the vessel sinking and the weather worsening, the eight man crew abandoned the former trawler at 1450hrs and took to the liferaft.

On arrival at the scene the rescue helicopter picked up the crew of the *St. Martin* from the liferaft, and took them to the James Paget Hospital in Gorleston for a check up.

The trawler LT376 *St. Martin* sets out on another fishing trip from Lowestoft.
Malcolm White Collection

A photograph supplied to Colne Shipping in 1991 of their vessel *St. Martin* sinking, and showing the crew boarding a liferaft.
Courtesy Colne Shipping (2000)

A selection of other fishing vessels with Lowestoft connections lost in the late 20th century

Lowestoft owned or registered vessels no longer in service due to reasons other than being life expired, scrapped, or being sold away from the port.

These vessels were generally considered to be part of the Lowestoft inshore fishing fleet although some may have ventured to more distant waters not usually considered as inshore fishing grounds.

Top Left - LT182 *Norfolk Spinner*
Bottom Left - LT419 *Jamesina* (as NN344)
Photographs copyright Malcolm White

Top Right - LT300 *St. Patrick* (as N185)
Bottom Right - LT596 *Boy Carl*
Photographs copyright Malcolm White

Date	Vessel	Description	Details of loss
1969 - January 29th	LT512 *Boy Alan*	Longshore	The owner of the 34ft. long *Boy Alan*, Mr. Arthur. F. Challis, was on the longshore boat when an explosion occurred on board whilst she was in the Hamilton Dock. Mr. Challis lost his life and the boat, new in 1966, was extensively damaged. The *Boy Alan* sank and was later dragged to where she could be beached while a decision was made concerning her future.
1969 - May 2nd	LT212 *Kastor*	Trawler	Indications that something was wrong followed the finding of wreckage from the *Kastor* off Ness Point and a lifebuoy from the vessel being picked up by LT478 *Winaway* in the same area. The body of the skipper (in a lifejacket) was recovered from the sea by LT325 *Sally*. *Kastor* was later found on the Cockle Shoal off Caister holed below the water line, the engine room flooded and the engine control set at full ahead. She broke up the next day and the mate's body was not found.
1974 - December 13th	R116 *Nikki*	Trawler	Vessel with three on board reported she was aground "three miles south of Cromer", later wreckage was found one mile north of Sea Palling and next day a body was found nearby. The other two persons on board were reported as missing.
1976 - June 5th	LT300 *St. Patrick*	Trawler	Following an explosion in her engine room 10 miles off Southwold, the vessel quickly filled with water. A Mayday distress call was transmitted and then the crew took to the liferaft. After drifting for about 10 hours the crew of three were picked up by the Dutch yacht *Woestduin* and landed at Lowestoft the next day.
1977 - March 28th	GY311 *Sioux*	Trawler	Whilst making for Grimsby from Lowestoft, the vessel ran into very bad weather and was overwhelmed off Spurn Head. The crew of five took to the liferaft and were later picked up by the standby safety vessel *Margaret Christina*. Skipper Norman Howe lost his life after assisting his crew to get into the liferaft, and then tried to jump into it. He missed the liferaft and was unfortunately swept away.
1979 - November 28th	LT419 *Jamesina*	Trawler	Problems with a sea cock led to the engine room flooding whilst fishing in the Outer Gabbard area. The vessel was taken in tow by LT351 *Michelle Louisa* but after about 30 minutes, the 72ft. *Jamesina* settled in the water and the tow was disconnected. She sank in around 18 fathoms of water about 18 miles north of the *Gabbard* Lightvessel.

Lowestoft Fishing Vessels Remembered - *Section Three*

Date	Vessel	Description	Details of loss
1980 - February 22nd	LT182 *Norfolk Spinner*	Trawler	Grounded on south breakwater at entrance to Aberdeen Harbour. Later the badly damaged vessel was salvaged and scrapped. Of the three man crew, there was one survivor who was taken to hospital but died shortly afterwards.
1983 - November 17th	LT596 *Boy Carl*	Trawler	Sprang a leak and sank near Smiths Knoll. The crew of five were rescued by the side trawler LT457 *Rosevear*.
1985 - January 22nd	LT197 *Pescoso II*	Beam Trawler	Sank approximate 100 miles east of the Humber. The crew took to the liferaft and the ferry *Dana Maxima* tried to rescue them but due to height of the vessel and the rough sea conditions, this was not possible. The crew were eventually picked up by helicopter and taken to Grimsby.
1986 - August 12th	TH35 *Pescado*	Beam Trawler	Capsized whilst hauling her fishing gear and sank north east of Shipwash Light Buoy. Of the four man crew, there was one survivor.
1990 - October 10th	BCK52 *Cornelia*	Beam Trawler	Sprang a leak and sank 22 miles south of Berry Head. The five persons on board were rescued by the beam trawler *Janie Marie*.

LT197 *Pescoso II*
Copyright Malcolm White

LT212 *Kastor*
Courtesy Ken Kent (1999)